The Black

*Where Women Pray
and Men Prey*

Deborrah Cooper

The Black Church:
Where Women Pray and Men Prey

©2012 Deborrah Cooper

Cover Design by
Tarryn Cooper

Edited by
Leslie J. Ansley
The Leslie Agency Inc.

©Deborrah Cooper/Amagination Publishing. All rights reserved. No part of this book may be used or reproduced in any manner whatsoever without written permission of the author, except in the case of brief quotations embodied in critical articles and reviews. Visit the author's website to submit your interview request online at www.womenpraymenprey.com.

ISBN 978-1-105-63687-5

To Natalie and Tarryn

May you never lose sight of the wonderful young women that you are… your existence is a blessing to the world.

To My Parents

I'm so glad you were ahead of your time. Thank you for providing the supportive environment that allowed me to define myself.

Contents

Preface

Acknowledgements

Introduction

Chapter 1

BLACK CHURCHES - THE PAST AND THE PRESENT

Definition of a Black Church 3
Churches Men Sexism and Civil Rights 7
The Era of Prosperity Gospel 10
Close Your Eyes and See Green 12

Chapter 2

FALSE PROMISES FROM FALSE PROPHETS

Like Shooting Fish in a Barrel 19
Church Women All Think the Same 20
Church or Cult – A Checklist of Warning Signs 26
Black Pastors as Religious Sociopaths 30
The Female Role in Black Churches 36
Church as the New Slave Master 44
Following and Worshipping Men, Not God 48
Pastor in Your Marital Bed 50

Chapter 3

MALE SAINTS AND FEMALE SINNERS

Religious Judgments of Female Sexuality 55
She Should Have Kept Her Legs Closed 57
She Tried to Trap Him 60
Enslavement of Women Through Child Bearing 63

Single Black Women as Jezebels 69
Lust and the Virtuous Woman 71

Chapter 4

PRAY, PAY AND OBEY!

The Most Religious Demographic in the U.S. 79
Christians and Female Submission 80
Domestic Violence and the Church 84

Chapter 5

THE SINGLE BLACK WOMAN IN CHURCH

Games of Romance Played on Single Women 91
Christianity – a Woman's Religion 96
What Going to Church Won't Do.................................. 97
Why Independent Black Women Settle for Less 104
Single Men are Not in Church and it's No Accident 1113
The 5 Types of Single Men That Go to Church 117
Marriage – The Carrot at the End of the Stick 121
Too Educated, Materialistic and Undesirable 125

Chapter 6

CHURCHIANITY - THE ONLY LEGITIMATE CON GAME IN TOWN

The Business of Churching.. 131
How Church is a Con Game 132
Pastors Using Your Fears Against You 133
Breaking Down the Pimp Game of Churching........... 136

Chapter 7
PULPIT PIMPS AND CONGREGATION HOs

P.I.M.P. Means Put it in My Pocket 146
The 10 Step Plan to Turning a Bitch Out 148
Pastors as Mack Pimps 157

Chapter 8
SEXUAL PREDATORS AND PREY

Pedophiles as Church Leaders.. 163
Youth Are at High Risk for Sexual Assault................. 173
The Predator's Game of Sexual Coercion................... 174
Predators in the Pews 177
Cognitive Brain Development in Teens 181
The Tricks of a Child Molester 183
How Child Molesters Groom Their Victims 184
What to do if you Suspect Sexual Abuse................... 187
Respect Your Little Person as an Individual............. 191
Abuse Awareness for Single Mothers 193

Chapter 9
THE WOLF IN SHEEP'S CLOTHING: FLEECING THE FLOCK

Christianity is Not a Religion, It's an Industry 199
Pastor Arranged Marriages for Profit......................... 209
Mega-Church= Mo Money, Mo Money 211

Conclusion 219

About the Author 225
Bibliography 229

Preface

The truth will set you free. But first it will piss you off. ~*Gloria Steinem*

The question has been asked repeatedly: "Why are there so many unmarried black women?" My position is that black churches and the men that run them are at the core of the problem of perpetual singleness for millions of African-American women.

Statistical comparisons in marriage rates between the races cannot be ignored. U.S. Census reports published in 2010 suggest that just 30.9 percent of blacks are married, which means 69.1 percent are not. By the time they reach 40 years of age, 31 percent of African American women have never been married at all, compared to just 9 percent of Caucasian women, 11 percent of Asian women and 12 percent of Hispanic women.

Mainstream media outlets such as the New York Times, The Washington Post, CNN, Nightline and ABC have been fixated on the high numbers of single black women in the U.S. for several years. White female newscasters practically gloated when reporting on the marital state of millions of black women. Their glee clearly inferred that black women are single because there is something wrong with them-- they don't measure up somehow; they are not worthy of having a husband like white women are.

Comedian-turned-relationships guru-turned-game show host Steve Harvey, actor Hill Harper, Sherri Shepherd (co-host of ABC's "The View"), Jacque Reid (then star of VH1's "Let's Talk About Pep") and Jimi Izrael (author of "The Denzel Principle") got together to discuss why educated, professional black women cannot find a man. The Nightline Face-Off -- W*hy Can't a*

Successful Black Woman Find a Man? - aired in April 2010. During that broadcast we heard even more criticism from the males on the panel about why black women remain unmarried. Hill Harper's suggestion was that black women should date men who show potential, despite their not necessarily having reached it yet. Jimi Izrael said that black women should lower their expectations and stop looking for a man so perfect he exists only in their imaginations.

The day after the show aired, the Internet exploded with posts by young black women, alarmed their dream of a loving husband and family might never come true. They wondered if Steve, Hill and Jimi were right and their standards *were* too high. Maybe they *were* too educated, too independent, too successful, too intimidating to men. Maybe they *should* lower their expectations and "work with a brotha" to lift him up and bring him along, just as Steve, Hill and Jimi had suggested.

Dismayed at the reaction of bright, young, black women to this negative propaganda, I thought I should spend a little time looking at the programs in more detail. My goal was to find the common denominator between millions of single black women and what might be the root cause of such widely disparate marriage statistics. Surely, women living in cities throughout the country, of varying backgrounds and ages, with different upbringings and levels of education had to have something in common besides being black, female and single.

I came up with two common denominators: (1) Each and every one of the black women interviewed proclaimed themselves to be Christian; and (2) Most of the black women interviewed said that they go to church. Anyone of even the most basic level of intelligence could see that if all of these people have just one common denominator that is where one should start looking for the problem.

Okay, so what then is going on in black churches across America? I asked hard questions and I got shocking answers, and subsequently published the findings on my blog Surviving Dating on June 24, 2010 in an article entitled *The Black Church – How Black Churches Keep African-American Women Single and Lonely*. Within a few days calls and emails from high-profile radio show hosts Tom Joyner, Michael Baisden and Rev. Al Sharpton came in, followed by dozens of interview requests by newspaper reporters and television producers, including CNN.

Readers of blogs across the web, as well as those that heard the radio and television interviews wrote in to relate their personal experiences in the church, anxious to continue the discussion. Thousands of email testimonials and comments about the black church article were submitted through the SurvivingDating.Com website, many of which appear in this book.

Throughout my entire career, I've embraced controversial topics, discussing them in a straightforward manner which upsets those unaccustomed to an outspoken and opinionated female. Anticipating some level of anger over my criticism of the church intentionally keeping black women single, I expected to hear controverting opinions; however, many comments were downright hostile. How could I, as an African-American woman, dare to question the goings-on of the black church? "You are just bitter and angry... you must have been hurt by someone in church" was always their inevitable conclusion. Staunchly defending their church and pastor no matter what, many (black women especially) proclaimed me to be a blasphemous child of

Satan attempting to divide the black community and turn women against God.

In reality, I have not been hurt by anything nor am I bitter either. I do not hate ministers or churches. I have not been hurt by a member of a church, no one in my family has been fleeced in a church, and I have not been used or sexually abused by a pastor or minister or bishop. By that same token, I am not a member of a church and refuse to become one, thus I have no particular loyalty to churches or anyone associated with a church. I stand alone, reporting in a dispassionate, rational manner the behaviors and attitudes that I've witnessed for the past 30 years amongst the African-American, church-going community.

The motivation behind the 2010 Black church article was to sound the alarm; to get black women to wake up and smell the stink of manipulative games and pimpery in the pulpit that kept them single and alone. Discussions subsequent to the publication of that piece alerted me to the very real need for this book.

Acknowledgements

No writer is inspired to create in a vacuum. We are all pushed to greatness by those that surround us with love, insight and supportive encouragement. You know who you are.

Many people contributed their secrets, frustrations and stories to this book through email and face-to-face interviews. Though these individuals are neither sociologists nor renown scientific researchers, their personal experiences make them the true experts. Each testimonial and story is extremely valuable and an important element of this work -- this project would not exist without you.

Finally, my parents and grandparents were influential in creating the woman that I have become. Though people around them condemned their refusal to make me be "a girl," they allowed me the freedom to be the untamed bull in the china shop I wanted to be. I relish thinking freely, breaking every mold and staid ideal that stands in my path to this day.

Introduction

Though the primary focus of this book is on the oft-ignored victimization of women and children in black churches, we must acknowledge that men get taken as well. However, this work reflects and focuses on statistics that show a marked imbalance in the number of women and children in churches as compared to males.

In his book *Why Men Hate Going to Church* author David Murow stated "women comprise more than 60 percent of the typical adult congregation on any given Sunday. At least one-fifth of married women regularly worship without their husbands." The Barna Group (a religious research group based in Ventura, California) reports that more than 90 percent of American men believe in God, with five out of six calling themselves Christian - but that only one-third of the men attend church on Sundays. (State of the Church Series, 2011). In summary, 60 percent or more of the attendees at American churches are female. Therefore, this book will focus on the demographic most affected by interactions with cunning religious leaders: women.

Messages delivered to black females in churches across the country keep them locked in fearful acceptance of their own abuse and dependency. Twisted scriptural mandates to be patient, to stay on their knees praying, to be of service to some pastor/minister and his church reduce women to nothing but bodies to be used to promote the pastor's acquisition of power and wealth.

Carter G. Woodson, author of the historic 1933 essay "The Miseducation of the Negro," wrote the following observation of black preachers and churches:

"The Negro church often fulfills a mission to the contrary of that for which it was established . . . it seems that practically all the incompetents and undesirables who have been barred from other walks of life by race prejudice and economic difficulties have rushed into the ministry for the exploitation of the people. Honest ministers who are trying to do their duty, then, find their task made difficult by these men who stoop to practically everything conceivable. Almost anybody of the lowest type may get into the Negro ministry."

Black women in churches across the country are being gamed on to support men executing the biggest con game and scam against females in existence. The ills suffered by women in black churches under patriarchal philosophies of male superiority are shocking.

Throughout the pages of this book are real stories about churches and the pastors that run them. These are true accounts of men charged with the spiritual enrichment and development of communities – behaving in damaging, abusive ways towards women and children. You will also be presented with information that encourages you to examine the operation and modern purposes of black churches, the messages given to you while in church and the reasons you maintain a membership in a club that may be doing you more harm than good.

There are several important questions that women should have solid answers to, thus every church-going woman should ask herself:

- Why am I going to church?
- Is what I am looking for my church to provide being offered within this environment?
- Am I being treated fairly and honestly by my church leaders?
- Is the true spirit of God as written in the Bible being represented on a daily basis by this church and its leaders?

Women have been quick to defend their churches, saying that *their* pastors aren't at all like those described in this text. They believe it should be made clear to readers that women are preyed on in non-black churches as well, and certainly not ALL black churches are bad. Though both statements may be correct, does such nit-picking really matter when millions of African-American women are being used, tricked and gamed on in their houses of worship? Why deflect from the key issues by turning our focus away the victims, diluting the message with excuses and exceptions to the rule?

Certainly there are some churches in black communities headed by men of honor that are more focused on spiritual enrichment and who work diligently to better the lives of their congregants and the surrounding community; however, I am saying those churches are in the minority. In the majority of cases, the black women staunchly defending their pastors are still asleep, having chosen to believe what they are told without question and without looking under the surface. This unquestioning belief is what the religious call "having faith."

All scriptural references in this text have been included for the sole purpose of illustrating contradictions between actual

Biblical text and the words spoken aloud by pastors as The Truth. My use of scriptural quotes should not be construed as personally endorsing or supporting such beliefs; they are utilized merely to demonstrate to you how the Word is distorted, and used to manipulate and control large numbers of people.

We are asleep until the moment we wake up. When asleep, a woman will not see what she needs to see, or understand what she needs to understand. Until the moment she awakens and opens her eyes to see churches and the people running them in a new light, a woman attending a dangerous church will not see the treacherous risks that lie before her.

As a social researcher, I write about a wide variety of subjects with a critical eye. My goal always has and always will be to expose uncomfortable truths in black culture and relationships. Whatever path you take in regards to church attendance is your choice alone to make. My job is only to awaken sleeping women that have blind faith in their religious leaders to the reality they may have ignored. Whatever they do with that reality is their affair.

The shocking first-hand accounts shared of abuses in the name of God are true; however all personally identifying information (such as age, location and church names) has been changed or omitted to protect privacy. The names used herein are not their real names.

If you are a single black woman regularly attending church and tithing, or you are a woman with children that accompany you to church, please open your mind to the expressed dangers within the walls of your house of worship, because far too often, black women go to church to pray to God, and black men are there to game on, feed on and prey on them like predators.

The Black Church

*Where Women Pray
and Men Prey*

DEBORRAH COOPER

www.womenpraymenprey.com

1

BLACK CHURCHES - THE PAST AND THE PRESENT

A brief overview of the history of the black church in America and how we got where we are today with religion

Religion is the sigh of the oppressed creature, the heart of a heartless world, and the soul of soulless conditions. It is the opium of the people.

~ Karl Marx (1818-1883)

Definition of a Black Church

Loosely, the term "black church" refers to Christian churches that serve predominantly African-American congregations. The late professor, C. Eric. Lincoln co-authored, *The Black Church in the African American Experience* with Lawrence Mamiya. They described the, "seven major historic black denominations: the African Methodist Episcopal (AME) Church; the African Methodist Episcopal Zion (AMEZ) Church; the Christian Methodist Episcopal (CME) Church; the National Baptist Convention, USA., Incorporated (NBC); the National Baptist Convention of America, Unincorporated (NBCA); the Progressive National Baptist Convention (PNBC); and the Church of God in Christ (COGIC)," as comprising "the black church."

However, to simplify things "the black church" means that (1) the leaders of the congregation are black; (2) the majority of the congregation is black; and (3) the church serves a largely black community. Whether protestant, Catholic, Jehovah's Witness or Seventh Day Adventist, those three components will designate a church as "a black church" for the purposes of this discussion. Though prayer and church were an integral component of African culture even before our enslaved ancestors landed on the shores of the U.S., our conversation will focus exclusively on the rise of the black church after the first slave ships arrived in America.

With the exception of the Quakers, every religious group in the U.S. used the Bible to justify and endorse the continued enslavement of black people. White slave masters used a twisted version of the Christian religion as a tool to control the actions of blacks and to keep them subservient and afraid of retribution. Not understanding what slaves were saying in their native tongues, fearful Whites prevented their slaves from gathering or holding any sort of spiritual services. Drum beating (used in Africa to send messages) was also banned. Whites were concerned that the slaves would use their religion or drums to coordinate efforts to plan escapes and/or uprisings against the slave owners.

Verses in the Old Testament were often quoted by slave owners which suggested that blacks were a people cursed by God; it was therefore their duty to be humbly obedient servants to whites. Southern states justified slavery with Ephesians 6:5 ("slaves, obey your earthly masters with fear and trembling"), or Titus 2:9 ("tell slaves to be submissive to their masters and to give satisfaction in every respect").

There are some inherent problems with this convenient thinking and selective choice of Scripture:

#1 "White" Christians assumed that the so-called "curse of Ham" (Genesis 9:25) was to cause Ham's descendents to be black, which therefore meant that they were cursed. While it may be likely that Africans are descendants of Ham (Cush, Phut, and Mizraim), it is not likely that they are descended from Canaan, and the curse was actually declared on Canaan, not Ham;

#2 There is no evidence from Genesis that the curse of Canaan has anything to do with skin color. Proponents of the slave trade argued that the "mark of Cain" in Genesis 4 was that he was turned black; however, there is no evidence of this in Scripture;

#3 The use of these biblical passages to equate dark skin with bad and evil is juxtaposed against the belief that white skin is good and pure. Considering the region of the world where the Bible stories originate, such an assumption is completely illogical and flies against the reality of the complexions of the inhabitants of the region; and

#4 According to the Bible, neither God nor Moses advocated slavery, counting slave traders and owners of slaves as the very worst sinners (1 Timothy 1:10 which admonishes kidnappers, men stealers and slave traders and Exodus 21:16 "…and he that stealeth a man, and selleth him, or if he be found in his hand, he shall surely be put to death").

Though many whites throughout the South resisted teaching their slaves about Christ, beginning in the mid-1700s, many slave owners began to bring in preachers to educate slaves on Christianity and uplift them from their "savagery." Those fearful of their slaves learning about the Bible were concerned that the slaves would read the texts and arrive at the conclusion that God was in favor of equality between the races. In particular, I believe their chief fear lay in Genesis 15:13-14 which references God freeing the Israelites:

13 Then He said to Abram: "Know certainly that your descendants will be strangers in a land that is not theirs, and will serve them, and they will afflict them four hundred years.

14 "And also the nation whom they serve I will judge; afterward they shall come out with great possessions."

Christianity spread through the plantations of the South with ease, as it provided hope – something all downtrodden people need. The hope that one would be happy in heaven for being prayerful and obedient, then blessed with eternal life in the land of milk and honey was irresistibly attractive to slaves. Following the masters religion provided slaves with a dream - an expectation that more and better than the painful, tortuous existence they were actually living would be their reward in the afterlife.

Though some white churches allowed slaves to worship in their church buildings, albeit seated in sections segregated from whites, church services for slaves generally took place outdoors. Sunday church meetings provided a mental and spiritual escape from the oppression of slavery, and strengthened their resolve to endure another week of back-breaking work and cruelty. Church was important to the slaves because it was the only place they could feel even remotely free.

Black churches boomed after the Civil War. Former slaves were able to take advantage of their new freedom to organize and minister to themselves without needing to be either secretive for fear of retribution, or under the supervision of a white church body as they had before emancipation. Members of black churches worked closely together, coordinating efforts to care for the sick and aged, sheltering travelers and providing financial assistance to deserving college students.

Black churches served many purposes after the civil war, including being used as schools, performing arts centers and community meeting halls until dedicated structures could be built. Within Black churches, members found a place to provide and receive emotional support, to share information, to resolve legal conflicts, and to organize for political action.

Churches have a long and proud history of bearing the cross for the black communities in which they stand; however that cross is cracked and crumbling.

Churches, Men, Sexism and the Civil Rights Movement

Churches were instrumental in organizing African Americans to fight for their civil rights in the late-1950s to mid-1960s. The church was, at that time, a powerful ally for aspiring black leaders to spread messages of hope and change as battles were waged for voting rights, eradication of Jim Crow, and elimination of segregation in schools and communities across the country.

The leadership role assumed by black churches in the civil rights movement made perfect sense due to their existing structure and function as the central gathering spot within most African-American neighborhoods. As such, black churches served as the link between whites and blacks in many regions of the country, as church leaders attempted to sooth racial tensions while encouraging blacks to participate in the political system and to wage war on discrimination.

In retaliation against this focus on increasing power and autonomy, angry mobs of whites burned down and firebombed dozens of black churches throughout the South. The most famous case happened in 1963. Four small children were killed in Birmingham, Alabama, when the Sixteenth Street Baptist Church was firebombed by members of the Ku Klux Klan. In one month in 1957, four black churches were bombed in

Montgomery, Alabama, with dozens of others burned in Tennessee, Arkansas, Alabama, Mississippi and Georgia over the following 10 years.

Black churches, together with black political leaders such as Stokely Carmichael, Whitney Young, Ralph Abernathy, Dr. Martin Luther King, Jr., and organizations like the Southern Christian Leadership Conference were instrumental in empowering African Americans and creating forward movement for our race as a whole. The combined social and political needs of African Americans caused a great deal of responsibility to fall on the shoulders of black ministers, and as such they wielded a great deal of power.

However the real movers of the civil rights movement that are rarely seen or discussed were the voices and faces of black women.

For example, the catalyst for the civil rights battle for desegregation was Rosa Parks who one day in 1955 decided she was tired and needed to sit down on her way home from work rather than give up her seat to a white man. The year-long boycott of the bus system in Montgomery, Alabama was organized and executed by black women, primarily domestic workers that had traveled to the homes of their employers in the back seats of busses for years. However, as soon as their efforts gained national attention and men like Martin Luther King, Jr. got involved, they systematically excluded women from prominent leadership roles and the limelight. Reportedly, Rosa Parks was denied the right to speak at the first mass meeting about the Montgomery bus boycott, dismissed by one of the ministers who said he thought she'd "done enough already."

Few black women civil rights activists besides Rosa Parks are recognized names. Though six of the Little Rock Nine -- the first black students to attend Central High School in Little Rock, Arkansas -- were female, we rarely hear their names. Few know or have even heard of the stories and contributions of Fannie Lou Hamer, Ella Baker, Vivian Malone Jones, Daisy Bates, Lillian Smith, Mamie Till-Mobley, Lorraine Hansberry, Dorothy Height and Septima Poinsette Clark. Most black women involved in the civil rights movement were in churches in the background – setting up chairs and tables, cooking for and cleaning up after rallies, organizing for the next ones... just anonymous faces in the crowds seen in black and white photos of the civil rights marches getting bitten by dogs, beaten by police, and shot down with high pressure water hoses.

Though black women were standing right along with black men during the civil rights battle of the 1960s, black women were actually fighting two battles: racism and sexism. While we were helping black men fight and win the battle of racism, black men's efforts were then and continue to be focused primarily on promoting their own agenda and advocating for themselves while merely giving lip service to advocating for and promoting the agenda and needs of black women.

When a black man believes that there is a double standard with regards to his behavior and accountability, he is treating black women exactly how the Klan treated him. When black men promote a belief system that places him in superior position to women based upon his belief that he has certain inalienable rights because he was born male, he is practicing sexism.

Sexism against women is the equivalent of racism against a person of color; black men with sexist attitudes and practices against women of color are no different than any redneck racist. The principle that men are the most important demographic in the black community is a mindset that permeates our culture to this day. Attitudes of this type of male dominance are especially prevalent in churches, where black women are willing participants in their own spiritual, emotional and economic downfall.

The Era of Prosperity Gospel

Again I tell you, it is easier for a camel to go through the eye of a needle than for a rich man to enter the kingdom of God (Matthew 19:24)

Modern churches are very different from the historically black churches our ancestors built. The black church's focus on spiritual and community growth changed when the use of Scriptures was set aside to focus on digging into the pockets of the congregants. The era of what is now called the "prosperity ministry" or "prosperity gospel" infiltrated black churches in the 1970s, reaching mainstream acceptance in the 1990s.

Dr. J. Alfred Smith, Jr., head pastor of Allen Temple Baptist Church (one of the largest churches in Oakland, California) was recently quoted as saying:

> *"Members of the Black Church are flocking to 'religious' leaders who are totally out of touch with the liberation agenda and who are wholeheartedly preaching greed as the 'new level' of spirituality to which they have transitioned. Black parishioners are interested in large gatherings of praise where Darfur, Sudan,*

Angola, the Congo, and Colombia never get mentioned. (They) are interested in large gatherings of praise where they can gather for an entire week of getting their praise on and getting their shout on, speaking in tongues and spending their dollars."

The prosperity concept derived from the belief that although Christians should stay mindful of access to heaven, God doesn't want his people to wait until they pass on to inherit his blessings. Money, say the prosperity ministers, isn't the root of all evil; it's the lack of money that is the root of all evil. The prosperity gospel is a frequently criticized theology that teaches wealth and health are signs of God's blessing, and that these blessings can be yours if the price is right.

Anthony Bradley is the author of *Keep Your Head Up: America's New Black Christian Leaders, Social Consciousness, and the Cosby Conversation*. In a March 2012 interview with The Gospel Coalition, he is quoted as saying:

"Sadly, the prosperity gospel has taken the already individualistic, consumeristic American understanding of what it means to follow Christ to a new destructive level. This is why we included a chapter on this movement. Its theologically poisonous tentacles have found their way into many black churches, and it is now a major force in the black expression of Christianity in America, Latin America, and Africa. Black pastors who are faithful to the Bible's theology and faithful to the gospel of Christ are burdened to regularly preach against the prosperity gospel because of its presence in so many black churches…"

During the civil rights era, Dr. Martin Luther King Jr. was the symbol of unity and religious purity to Christians of all races. Yet, in 2008 (40 years after his death), CNN reported:

> "The contemporary white church has largely accepted King as a religious hero. Yet some observers say there is one religious community that continues to shun King -- the black church. Dr. King remains a prophet without honor in the institution that nurtured him, some black preachers and scholars say.
>
> "They also say King's 'prophetic' model of ministry -- one that confronted political and economic institutions of power -- has been sidelined by the prosperity gospel.
>
> "Prosperity ministers preach that God rewards the faithful with wealth and spiritual power. Prosperity pastors such as Bishop T.D. Jakes have become the most popular preachers in the black church. They've also become brands. They've built mega churches and business empires with the prosperity message."

Close Your Eyes and See Green!

Rev. Frederick J. Eikerenkoetter II, the flamboyant minister referred to as "Reverend Ike" was one of the first to begin preaching the message of what he called the "Prosperity Now" gospel to African Americans. Though he never claimed to be a Christian minister, Eikerenkoetter built and headed the United Church Science of Living Institute in New York for several decades. He was quoted in a 1972 issue of the *New York Times* as saying:

> *"Close your eyes and see green! Money up to your armpits, a roomful of money and there you are, just tossing around in it like a swimming pool."*

The first black preacher to be televised (Jim Bakker, Pat Robertson and Jimmy Swaggart were all white), Rev. Ike raked in millions by requesting donations in cash from the viewing audience. The wearing of flashy jewelry, expensive clothing and several luxury cars soon followed. "My garages runneth over," he observed.

Using a combination of wit, humor and Scripture in his presentations, Reverend Ike drew standing-room-only crowds everywhere he preached. He often cited Matthew by wisecracking: "If it's that difficult for a rich man to get into heaven, think how terrible it must be for a poor man to get in. He doesn't even have a bribe for the gatekeeper."

Though he died in 2009, Rev. Ike's money hustle was working even after death. "In lieu of flowers, Rev. Ike would ask that tributes and/or Offerings be sent to: Rev. Ike Ministries."

Though he was the first internationally known black televangelist, Rev. Ike has been joined by dozens of other multi-millionaire preachers over the four decades. Each preaches his message to multitudes of black women, who give these guys huge sums of money without asking for anything in return.

The prosperity ministry twists the message of Jesus Christ into a message of salvation achieved through wealth and prosperity, but only if one gets right with God by giving money to the church. The message Christians receive is that they are somehow magically immune from human suffering, sickness, or pain through an exemption clause received by "planting your seed." In other words, if you plant the appropriate number of C-note seeds, you will receive a financial blessing. The implication is that one's "voluntary donations" to a church should be considered an investment upon which you will receive a guaranteed return.

Prosperity ministries led by Creflo "Gimme Your Last" Dollar, Frederick "The" Price "is Never Too High for Blessings", Leroy "Big Pimpin" Thompson, and T. D. "Take Dat Money" Jakes are broadcast across cable and satellite television airwaves weekly. The popularity of television in black homes has turned local prosperity preachers into religious celebrities that have groupies around the world, just like any hip hop music artist. Jakes' Potter's House is broadcast into hundreds of prisons in 30 states on Wednesday nights, facilitated by the purchase of satellite dishes paid for by his church for any prison that needs one.

Jonathan L. Walton, an assistant professor of African-American religion at Harvard Divinity School was recently quoted as saying:

> "They're pastors, but they're really in the Halloween costume of a Fortune 500 CEO. And in the process they're trick-or-treating the people."

No longer focused on morality and following the teachings of Christ, the prosperity ministry is a movement and theology that once seemed like an aberrant anomaly. However, pushing financial prosperity over spiritual prosperity has become the chief focus of a number of scandalous black preachers.

2

FALSE PROMISES FROM FALSE PROPHETS

How women are brainwashed and their thinking manipulated in black churches though 'faith'

When it comes to controlling human beings, there is no better instrument than lies. Because you see, humans live by beliefs. And beliefs can be manipulated. The power to manipulate beliefs is the only thing that counts. ~Michael Ende

Like Shooting Fish in a Barrel

Black women have an inordinate amount of faith in both black men and black churches. My position is that such blind and unwavering faith in either is misplaced. It is my belief that the black church, structured around traditional gender roles that make women submissive to and inferior to men, greatly limits females. Single black women sitting in church every Sunday are being subtly brainwashed, soothed and placated into waiting without demand for what they want to magically come to them. Who is doing this to black women? The male standing at the front of the church in the role of spiritual leader, that's who!

It's beneficial to the church to keep the female congregation confused and wanting with a three-step program: (1) Make the women believe they need to be led by a man; (2) brainwash the people you can get under your influence and control; and (3) ostracize the people you can't.

Black women tend to be unquestionably trusting when it comes to their churches, the church members, and their pastors. A yearning to see only the good in others is at the root of many issues and problems suffered by black women in churches. When women become excessively emotionally or psychologically attached to their pastors, they will, with an almost addictive fervor, do anything possible to defend the very men that are robbing them blind and preying on them like rabid wolves.

Church Women All Think the Same

There is a certain mindset that women steeped in religion seem to have which men laughingly call "acting brand new" or "gullible." From their perspectives on life to their belief systems about men and love, right and wrong, women that proclaim to be very religious are astonishingly similar. Few express curiosity about or a willingness to expand their horizons beyond the lifestyle, people, places and even foods they are familiar with.

Fear is prevalent in the lives of most women to a certain degree, but the church woman is consumed by fear; the threat of God's wrath and damnation are reflected in every decision she makes. Fear of dire consequences should she dare to behave in a way that demonstrates initiative, pride, defiance or novelty locks timid church women into fearful lives of inaction. Many adopt an attitude of learned helplessness, shockingly similar to that of a female slave. The only difference is that her new master is a wrathful God, the dominating overseer is the pastor, and the threatened punishment for disobedience is not the whip, but eternal hell.

Though women in churches will proudly state that they are "an independent black woman" many men feel there is nothing independent about their thinking at all.

> "Black women need to stop believing in so much b.s. Once a man knows that you are a 'church girl,' you are so easy to figure out. To a man that knows anything about human nature you are like taking candy from a baby. Them sistahs set themselves up to be used as jump offs. If church is your crutch, then you'll be handicapped for

life in the real world. I can't stand it when I see them acting like they don't have a clue, even my own sisters. I think that is why so many black women in church get played used and dumped. Church is a players playground full of gaming-ass men and stupid-ass women." ~ Clifford W.

Examples of group think:

<u>Caring Only About Church-Related Causes</u>. Church women only care about what their church tells them is important to care about. If its orphaned children in Africa this year, they throw their energy into planning a trip to Africa and raising funds for the church to travel there and donate funds to African orphans. Yet, black American children without family, sitting in foster care right in their own neighborhood or city are completely ignored.

<u>Attending Only Church-Related Events.</u> Church women only go where their church tells them it's okay to go. They go by the busload to Christian gospel music fests, and T.D. Jakes or Tyler Perry plays. Many won't place themselves in any environment where alcohol is served (even if they aren't drinking it), and will therefore refuse to go to anything fun like a bowling alley, a sporting event, or a quality restaurant because people are drinking.

> "If you want a church girl all you gotta do is tote a Bible and say you love the Lord and they will be all over you like flies on sh*t. It's sad cuz those same sistahs talkin bout they 'waiting on the Lord' will run a brotha like me out the church tryna get him to marry her. Single black men are so rare in church, he can pretty much take

his pick. The church is full of horny, desperate women looking for that one single brother who 'loves the Lord.' I've seen many of these brothers using this to their advantage by being with multiple women at the same time." ~Delano J.

Dating Only Those That Pastor Thinks is Okay. There are Christian women who will only date men their pastor approves of. Giving a man you don't know this type of power enables him to set you up to be gamed on and used, and most of the time that's exactly what happens. (I'll explain some other tricks pastors use with mate selection further along.) Since most pastors are married and certainly not related to congregants, it's shocking that a grown woman of "independent mind" would allow him to decide who she dates or marries.

"I was up in church and we had altar call. I went up and several other people went up too. Now I have already noticed the looks I get from many of the men in my church but I ignore it. There is no one there that I want. Anyways I went up and this guy who is a member and has been watching me for awhile immediately went up and grabbed my hand as we stood before the altar. It didn't matter to me since everyone had to hold hands. (This guy is nice looking dark skinned with a muscular build, and bald.)

"So, after the prayer was finished and everyone returned to their seats, my so called 'pastor' got up and did his sermon. One of the things he said was 'I know you're looking at that beautiful woman and you want her, but she's not for you. Young lady. I know you're looking at that man with his dark skin and bald head and thinking he's so fine, but he's not for you.' I was thinking 'Wait what???' I thought it was a coincidence and I was kinda confused as to how it played into the sermon but I let it be.

"A few weeks after that I came to church and couldn't help but notice how my pastor seemed to make a whole lot of eye contact with me from the pulpit. He said during this sermon, 'You are the finest I have ever seen!' and I am still confused as to how this played into the sermon as well, but I ignored it again.

"A few weeks later I had to meet with my pastor as I am active in my church and I had some concerns. He fixed everything and I went away thinking my pastor is the best. However, that's when the calls and texting started. He began calling me 'baby' and telling me how he's been watching me for years and thinks I am 'beautiful' and 'hot.' Pastor got shut down with a swiftness. He's asked me out several times and he has been rebuked by me each and every time. I stopped attending his church. I saved each and every text message he sent, and I will pull his card before the entire city if he tries to get crazy because he didn't get his way with me." ~Tammy S.

Speak Only in Church-Related Phrases. Have you not noticed that religious black women sprinkle every conversation with the name of their pastor, or they say praise Jesus, or Lord blessed me, or thank you Jesus, etc., all day long? It's impossible to have a conversation with her that does not contain some reference to

23

one of those three entities. Even if she is at work helping customers, she completes her transactions with "have a blessed day!" or says, "God bless!" when she hangs up the telephone. Favorite phrases of black church women demonstrate a belief in powerlessness, in weakness, and acceptance that they are incapable of effectuating change on their own behalf. "I'm in between blessings right now!" or "I'mma just turn it over to God!" or "I put it in God's hands!" are presented as viable solutions instead of taking decisive action.

Church ladies go the same places, eat the same food, read the same books, buy the same clothes and spout the same trite phrases all the time; each is like a Stepford Wives replica of another.

The manufacturing of replicas in thinking and behavior via church rhetoric is intentional. When a pastor has a flock of women in his church that all think, behave and believe similarly – with the same fears and desires – they are much easier to influence and extremely easy to control.

Church women have been trained to get a feeling of comfort in routine sameness, and easily settle into a contented rut. Each is comfortable being around the same people, doing the same things, hearing the same messages year in and year out in church. However, if you never expose your mind to that which is new and different, how will you ever grow as a person outside the confines of your religion?

> "I love the Lord, but I believe that the black church has systematically brainwashed black woman to 'wait' on the Lord. There are 40-, 50-, 60-year-old women still

'waiting.' Is that God? I have to say no. Is it natural to wait 30 years for companionship? No! The black church promotes 'waiting' on the Lord theology because they know that women make up 75 percent of the tithing congregation. I went to a church that frequently encouraged the women to 'wait on the Lord' and these women were well into their 50s and 60s. This is not God. Let me say it again, THIS IS NOT GOD!!!

"The Lord desires that we live a balanced life and not in bondage to man's idea of church. There is so much to experience in the world but you cannot experience it holed up in the church from Sunday to Sunday. I say experience life and see God move in your life in a new way. Maybe then black women will be open to new experiences and meeting men that they would never have considered before." ~ Lisa M.

The unavoidable conclusion is that confining the growth and limiting the expansion of his female congregation's thinking is one of the chief goals of the religious leaders of many black churches. Reinforced is the belief that humans, (especially women), are nothing but flawed sinners – weak and powerless. Church rhetoric encourages adult women in child-like thinking, and discourages belief in a woman's power to personally affect her reality. Giving over total control of what she thinks, does and says to the charismatic religious leader (the pastor) creates a dangerous, cult-like environment.

Church or Cult? A Checklist of Warning Signs

❑ *Loss of individuality.* Individual identity, the group, the leader and/or God as distinct and separate categories of existence become increasingly blurred. Instead, in the follower's mind, these identities become substantially and increasingly fused as that person's involvement with the group/leader continues and deepens. Expressing thoughts, opinions or beliefs outside of those promoted by the leader is denounced as going against God. Critical thinking is discouraged as prideful and sinful; blind acceptance of the pastor's words is encouraged as "having faith."

❑ *Your salvation depends upon participation the group.* Unreasonable fear about the outside world, such as impending catastrophe, evil conspiracies and persecutions is common. Anyone considered an outsider may be viewed as not being a "real" Christian; therefore relationships with extended family, long-time friends and sometimes even adult children outside the influence of the leader are discouraged.

❑ *You feel pressured to give everything you have.* Some churches have four or more collections during every service. Church members are simultaneously pressured to tithe, donate for special funds and projects, and provide services of a personal nature to the pastor and other church leaders. Intimidation and fear of "looking bad" or viewed as being selfish is often enough to motivate meeker members to over-give their personal or financial resources.

- *The leader is the exclusive means of knowing "truth" or receiving validation, no other process of discovery is really acceptable or credible.* Takes liberties with scriptural interpretations, putting his own spin on them. Biblical passages which contradict unorthodox beliefs are twisted and taken out of context. Strong emphasis is placed upon certain passages making them their focus in ministry, while other pertinent Scriptures on essentials and practice are completely ignored. Biblical scholars who give a different interpretation are ignored or ridiculed.
- *Absolute authoritanism without meaningful accountability.* The group is focused on a single leader to whom group members display eager, almost obsessive commitment. His leadership or actions are never questioned or doubted; expressing any doubts is seen as a sign of disloyalty. No tolerance for questions or critical inquiry. Anything the leader does can be justified no matter how harsh or harmful.
- *The leader constructs a long list of rules and regulations.* He dictates exactly how group members must think, behave and feel. He places himself in the role of Father, requiring members to get permission from him to date, marry or change careers. Leaders may also determine the types of clothing members wear, how they discipline their children, educational achievements, and even where they live.
- *Guilt and shame* are frequently used as a way to control members, with the goal of inducing or creating confusion, fear, or doubt (i.e. "if that isn't working it means you are not praying hard enough … you are not walking the walk that Jesus instructed!")

Members feel like if there are ever problems, it is somehow their fault, never the responsibility of the group leaders.
- *Followers feel they can never be "good enough".* Followers are obligated to perform work to earn their way into God's favor (aka their leader). Service in the form of work for the church or leader is an essential requirement for salvation. However, no matter what you do, it is never enough.
- *Money collected from the group members is not used to benefit the group,* surrounding community or society at large; instead, signs of excessive spending and luxurious living is evident only in the lifestyle of the group leader(s).
- *Leader creates a false sense of righteousness and perfection* by repeatedly pointing out the horrors of the outside world and the shortcomings of non-members of the group or other religions. Intentionally creates unreasonable fears by threatening impending doom, catastrophic loss of life and property, or Satan-based persecutions unless desired actions are taken.
- *Deliberately withholds vital information from the group, or may outright lie.* No financial disclosure regarding budget, expenses, debts or other spending. Group members give without having any idea where their money is going. No independent third-party accounting or audited financial records.

(Based upon The Ten Warning Signs of a Potentially Unsafe Group/Leader and Ten Warning Signs Regarding People Involved With a Potentially Unsafe Leader developed by Rick Ross, Intervention Specialist. Used by permission of author)

Any one of these signs alone don't necessarily mean that your church is a cult or has cult-like tendencies. However, if three or more of these signs are present in your church environment, it would be prudent to take the matter seriously. Only a fool dismisses warnings -the wise (wo)man learns to properly interpret them.

I remember reading *Ain't I a Woman*, a transcript of a speech given by Soujourner Truth in 1881. An account of the speech by Frances Gage shares Truth's conviction about women's strength and power:

> "Den dat little man in black dar, he say women can't have as much rights as men, 'cause Christ wan't a woman! Whar did your Christ come from?" Rolling thunder couldn't have stilled that crowd, as did those deep, wonderful tones, as she stood there with outstretched arms and eyes of fire. Raising her voice still louder, she repeated, "Whar did your Christ come from? From God and a woman! Man had nothin' to do wid Him!"

When a pastor's female flock sees him and men in general as strong and powerful leaders to be followed, he can easily herd them in the direction he wants them to go. A deep-seated fear of garnering their Pastor's disapproval and fear of public ridicule and humiliation keep the female sheep in line.

From a few words spoken from his pulpit, a pastor can bring hundreds (if not thousands) of women joy by granting his approval, or he can bring them to their knees in supplication with guilt, confusion and shame. When a pastor is a master at speaking to the emotional hungers that his female members feel, he can adeptly use their needs against them to get what he wants, preying on their weaknesses like a hungry wolf.

The female sheep mistakenly believe that their pastor is there to herd, protect and take care of them, and minister to their needs as a shepherd does over his flock. The wolf is aware of this need and uses it to his advantage. While he expresses love and concern, and presents himself as seeking to help others, he is actually focused only on helping himself. He preaches with such dynamism and charisma that the flock believes every word he says. The controlling, deceitful behaviors exhibited toward women exposes many religious leaders as nothing but sinister sociopaths.

Black Pastors as Religious Sociopaths

Sociopaths are afflicted with what psychologists refer to as "antisocial personality disorder" -- a chronic mental sickness manifested in a blatant disregard for and repeated violation of the rights of others. Sociopaths have no conscience, and no real respect for right and wrong. Deception and manipulation are part of their daily interactions with other people. An inability to love or have meaningful interpersonal relationships is common amongst sociopaths; relationships to them are merely tools to get whatever it is they want from you.

In spite of the fact that many black women judge a man based upon how he is dressed and how he "looks", it is impossible to determine a sociopath by his appearance. Their attire is always well put together; they are usually very well groomed and quite charming. People who do revolting things do not usually look like they're bad. There is no "face of evil." These guys are also consummate actors, so sociopaths usually raise little suspicion at first glance. However, by knowing the signs to look for, it can become much easier for you to recognize when a religious leader is exhibiting traits of a sociopath. The following list provides a summary of the common behaviors exhibited by the religious sociopath:

- Slick Superficial Charm

Words are spoken in a smooth, easy manner. He appears to be quite fluent with language, which appeals to women's auditory nature. Very conventional boy-next-door or professional appearance. Charming and polite, he may come across as too good to be true – which he is.

- Manipulative Con Artist

He never recognizes the rights of others and sees his self-serving behaviors as permissible. He appears to be charming, yet is covertly hostile and dictatorial, seeing his victim as merely an instrument to be used. He may dominate and humiliate his victims. Ultimate goal is the creation of a willing victim that provides affirmation (respect, gratitude and love). Seeks to totally enslave his victims.

- Pompous Sense of Self

Feels entitled to certain things as his "right." Authoritarian and domineering; exercises tyrannical control over every aspect of the victim's life. Suffers from extreme narcissism and a grandiose sense of self-importance. May state jokingly that his goal is to rule the world -- except it's not a joke.

- Pathological Liar

He has no problem lying smoothly and easily, and it is almost impossible for him to be truthful on a consistent basis. Can create and get caught up in a complex web of lies about his own superpowers and inflated abilities. Is able to anticipate

and say with credibility exactly what people want to hear. Extremely convincing, even able to pass lie detector tests.
- Inordinately Focused on Sex

Sociopaths tend to be keenly focused on sexuality and are often hypersexual and promiscuous. The more taboo the manifestation of sexuality, the more attractive it is for the sociopath. Expends a great deal of time and energy talking about and engaging in many different forms of amoral sex. Promiscuity despite being married, child sexual abuse, rape and sexual acting out of all sorts is common. Likely to protect anyone accused of or suspected of sexual abuse or pedophile activity, and will obstruct criminal investigations into that person. This obsessive preoccupation with sexuality and normalizing socially unacceptable expressions of sex is a common trait of sociopaths.

- Incapable of Feeling Remorse, Shame or Guilt

A deep-seated rage (often at women), which is split off and repressed, is at the core. Paranoid. Does not see others around him as people, but only as targets and opportunities. Instead of friends, he has victims and accomplices who ultimately end up being victims. The end always justifies the means in his mind, and he lets nothing stand in his way.

- Displays Shallow Emotions

All displays of emotion have an ulterior motive designed to make you give to him. When he shows what seems to be warmth, joy, love and compassion it is more feigned than genuine. Outraged by insignificant matters, yet unmoved and cold by what would upset a normal person. Since he is not genuine, neither are his promises.

- Incapable of Loving

He possesses a self-centeredness that is resolute and unwavering. Incapable of human attachment to another person. Sociopaths and psychopaths are skillful at pretending a love for women or simulating parental devotion to children that they do not feel. The male sociopath convinces women they are in love with him and despite being treated callously, they blindly continue to be loyal to him and willingly cater to his every demand.

- Scapegoat and Blame Shift

Sociopaths are incapable of having the insight or willingness to accept responsibility for anything they do. Whatever the problem, it is always the fault of someone else. Highly skilled at redirecting all accusations and attempts at accountability back onto their accusers. Does not perceive that anything is wrong with him or his actions; the problem is always you.

- Fanatical Need for Stimulation

Enjoys living on the edge and taking wild risks with his health, money, and life. If you are tied to him, he will take the same risks with you. Verbal outbursts and physical confrontations are common. Promiscuity and gambling are familiar outlets as well.

- Callousness/Lack of Empathy

Unable to empathize with the pain of his victims, having only contempt for others' feelings of distress and readily takes advantage of them. Exploits anyone who displays vulnerability.

- Poor Behavioral Controls and Extremely Impulsive

Rage and abuse, alternating with small expressions of love and approval produce an addictive cycle for abuser and abused, as well as creating hopelessness in the victim. Believes he is all-powerful, all-knowing, entitled to every wish; displays no sense of personal boundaries and no concern for his impact on others.

- Early Behavior Problems or Juvenile Delinquency

He usually has a history of behavioral and academic difficulties beginning in early teens, yet "gets by" by conning others. Problems in making and keeping friends; aberrant behaviors such as cruelty to people or animals, stealing, arson, etc. are common.

- Irresponsible and Unreliable

Not concerned about wrecking other people's lives and dreams. Oblivious or indifferent to the devastation he causes. Does not accept blame himself, but blames others, even for acts he obviously committed.

- Parasitic Lifestyle with No Real Life Plan

Tends to move around a lot or makes all encompassing promises for the future; poor personal work ethic, but effectively exploits and lives off others.

- Criminal or Entrepreneurial Versatility

Likely to be illegally diverting or embezzling significant sums of church money to his own wallet, project, account or cause. Changes his image as needed to avoid prosecution. Changes life story readily to gain the upper hand in every situation. Possesses a wide range of criminal talents.

Entering into any type of relationship with a sociopath can be physically, emotionally and even financially draining. You will never have a truly honest, mutually interdependent relationship with a sociopath. In their relationships you give and they take.

> "Women are a game for most men. However, black men hit below the belt by leaving us feeling as used and abandoned as a corpse. I have dated the gamut of black men - the dope boy, the call-center clerk, a Sunday-go-to-meetin' Deacon, the engineer and the doctor - and they

are all the same. Black men (like a sociopath) cannot connect with anyone but themselves. There seems to be little to no investment in anything beyond a little roll in the hay with a curvy woman. That is shortsighted in a way that is detrimental to the generations to come. Sistahs are doing great things in this world and I can't understand why a black man is not elated to invest in that. Stop using and abusing our pride and spirits; stop being greedy, narrow-minded and opportunistic. Until we are held with esteem and perceived as fragile and essential to the collective black legacy we will all stay socially stunted, hurt and always arguing." ~ Jaycee S.

Women, ever hopeful denizens of faith, need to understand the most important thing when dealing with a sociopath is that they will never change into the man you hope they will become. No matter how much you love them, how long you stay with them, how many children you have by them, how much you defend them against other people, how much money you give them, how devoted you are to them or how many tears you shed, they will remain unmoved.

The black woman's belief that men only treat you the way you let them treat you plays into the sociopath's hands, perfectly. When women assume blame for how men treat them, it means the sociopath will never have to accept being held accountable nor take responsibility for the pain they cause. Black women are all too anxious to cover for the sociopath with excuse after excuse while faulting the victim for the abuses she suffered.

"I understand that the dating game requires a 'hunter instinct' in men, but black men have proven themselves beyond average hunters and are instead predators. I find their behavior coinciding with cold-blooded robbers and killers of the female fragility, self-esteem, spirit and in some cases overall potential. There is something quite peculiar about the black man's inability and/or desire to connect and build for the sake of happiness, even though they claimed themselves to be Christians like my family. I often contemplate if it is an actual inability or is it apathy towards desire or, much worse, just a game. What they unnecessarily leave behind without guilt or remorse is the remains of emotionally disfigured and disillusioned women." ~ Aribella M.

The Female Role in Black Churches

Negroes - Sweet and docile, meek, humble, and kind… beware the day they change their mind. ~Langston Hughes

In the male-dominated patriarchal culture of the black church, single women and widows have little to no authority. The religious leaders in black churches establish and maintain a social system where men are seen as the prize instead of women, and a standard (which women have bought into) where men have the sole power to determine a woman's value and rights.

Women in churches derive their influence based upon how important their husband or father is, and what position he carries in the church. Married women are at the top of the church-structure totem pole. Believing a married woman is somehow more important and better than a single woman is one reason why singles across the country are so anxious to be married:

They long to see what it feels like to have that type of power and respect.

> "When I was growing up in church, the best thing to be was a wife. You got to go around and make statements like 'my husband says' or 'let me ask my husband', all showing that you were the best woman ever because a man claimed you. I think it shows how low we as women have been socialized, because women only feel important and worthwhile if a man wants, claims and owns them. And once they get into it, they would rather stay than to be by themselves, because being owned/married ties into their self esteem soooo much. I'm SO GLAD I have been delivered out of that mindset!" ~Barbara N.

Married women are also viewed as more pure and virtuous in black churches. Having the title of "Mrs." within the church hierarchy is important for recognition and social standing. If her husband is an assistant pastor, deacon, a board member or other official in the church, she is almost revered by the other females. The queen bee in any black church is always the First Lady – the wife of the pastor or minister.

> "I remember being single and feeling a bit inferior to the marrieds. Remember I was in a church, and there was the singles ministry and the 'couples' ministry... I would always remember them making fun and giggling like the single people were not privy to the information that these 'Happy Couples' had. It was as if being connected is what will make you a better person. I hated it! THEN, when the young ladies would get married, a great amount of

other women would be seriously hating on them... like they won some prize. Even when I was NOT a church girl I had friends who would disappear when they got a man, like life had somehow just begun. I never did and still don't understand that." ~Shandra F.

Though there are increasing numbers of female head pastors in black churches across the country, the actual percentage is miniscule. Most black churches are very traditional and cannot see women as qualified to lead a ministry because women are supposed to be in a submissive, helpful role to men. Quoting 1 Corinthians 14:33-35: *"As in all the churches of the saints, let the women keep silence in the churches: for it is not permitted unto them to speak; but let them be in subjection, as also saith the law. And if they would learn anything, let them ask their own husbands at home: for it is shameful for a woman to speak in the church."*

This is why it is usually a married man (a husband) who is the church leader, pastor or minister, while the wife's role is to support her husband. So women are given titles such as pastors in training, junior pastors, or limited to being ministers of the youth or women's ministry.

Is this an absolute across the board rule? Of course not! As we've moved in the 21st century, there are more and more women at the helm of churches serving all nationalities. Have you noticed, however, that when a woman does lead a black church, she is normally a mature woman in her 50s or above? Oftentimes she is a widow who had a long-term, successful marriage before the death of her husband. The fact that she WAS married in the past gives her the required credibility and a pass to at least a modicum of authority. Black men readily discredit a woman from having any authority to speak on anything if she is not now, or has never been married. In their minds, unless you have been the property of another man, you as a woman have no credibility: You aren't good enough because no man "wanted" you.

Traditionally, the women in black churches (both single and married) are assigned menial, supportive tasks such as cleaning the church, taking care of young children during church services, or singing as a member of the choir. A woman with special skills in writing or playing music or with computer software may serve as the church organist or pianist, or perform administrative secretarial work for the pastor. What you will rarely see in a black church is a divorced woman or a never-married single mother being allowed to minister in any manner, especially in a leadership role.

Single, never-married women with children or divorced single moms are also the source of much apprehension among the married women in the congregation. The unmarried women are viewed as fornicators – women who have failed themselves and God by succumbing to sinful lusts of the flesh. Others may think they are in church only to find and hook up with some other woman's husband. The women and their children are gossiped about, maligned with harsh judgments and seen as dysfunctional, bastards or worst.

No one ascribes any judgmental traits to the single men or single fathers that come to church, however.

> "Not that I am promoting single parenthood, but referring to these households as 'broken' is offensive and

part of the problem. How about those 'broken' marital relationships in Christian-inspired, two-parent households? Being Christian doesn't inherently improve your relationship or parenting skills! I personally know plenty of screwed up Christian parents and children, people who can quote Scripture but can't digest it in any coherent, logical or critical way. When I go to church, I see 'sins' all around me, from the obviously gay minister of music to the less-than-tolerant minister, to the lying cut-throat gossiping men and women struggling for recognition and power at all costs. So many Christians crack me up because they want to prioritize others' sins over their own. The church should be inviting to ALL. I'm really starting to understand why many decide a Christian lifestyle is not for them. Who needs all the judgment preaching AT YOU attitude, especially when it's clear that the judgers' shit stinks like hell?" ~ Kevon N.

A woman that divorces her husband due to adultery or abuse will be given no acknowledgement or support by the church members for leaving. Instead, she is condemned as a rebellious, hard-headed black woman that refused to submit to her husband's authority, which in their minds may be justification for hitting her. When the split is announced, the tongue-wagging begins. Women in the estranged wife's family usually do all they can to convince her to return to the abuser with the goal of saving the marriage.

"I have, sadly, seen women who were sent back to losers by older female family members. There are plenty of people from past generations who are so marriage-oriented -- either by religion or old family values, which are still based on religion. When I was in Louisiana I met two old black women who bragged about what a good job they did, sending their granddaughter/niece back to an abusive, loser of a man with no job who cheated on her. They said that's what's wrong with my generation -- we are so quick to just give up and leave. One said her granddaughter needed to go back and support this loser in his time of need, and that it was her fault he cheated because he felt unloved by her. Then they had a big-ass fight and she packed her and her sons stuff and drove to Grandmas house an hour away. Grandma turned her right back around and said go home and fix her relationship with the emotional abuser." ~ Millie B.

The abused wife is also likely to witness sneering glances and hear other women snarl that her refusal to submit is why she was beaten. The insinuations are that her man cheated because he was "forced to get his needs met elsewhere"; that there was something she either didn't do or didn't do often enough, or was doing wrong. That's why "no man wants her" and she cannot "keep a man" – two hateful charges that women lob at each other like hand grenades.

Similarly, when a man cheats on his wife, she along with the other women in the congregation, blame and attack the woman he cheated with. The fact that a marriage failed due to a husband's betrayal, abandonment, abuse or mistreatment is blamed exclusively on the female or females involved. Not knowing what lies he may have told about his marital status and availability, the woman is deemed the sole party responsible in their eyes for a husband cheating – it's never the fault of the cheater.

I've heard such tales as a pastor saying from the pulpit, *"When I go out of town, my wife 'takes care' of me before I leave and when I come back. She knows her role. How can I desire to eat at 'Wendy's' when I have a home-cooked meal. Wives, you have to take care of that man."* When a woman's man cheats on her, the other woman is labeled a "home wrecker", while the man again gets a pass from breaking his marital vows and wrecking his OWN home.

In contrast, a divorced man will be accepted and embraced by the females of the congregation much more quickly than a divorced woman. Doesn't matter if he admits that the ruination of the marriage was 100 percent his fault, the sins he committed are magically forgiven. He can even remarry from within the flock (as the single women see "husband" on his forehead and move in before the ink is even dry on his divorce decree), and be invited to go into ministry. The women will still follow and respect HIM, though they shun and talk badly about the woman he mistreated.

Men also are able to, if single, continue to minister and remain in leadership roles as unmarried men with children on the way. Rarely are men brought in front of the church to apologize for their sin of getting a woman pregnant out of wedlock.

This problem of female acceptance is exacerbated should a woman demand fair treatment by asking church leaders some very hard questions.

"From the time I was about 15 or 16 every question I had about faith and life was met with censure or ridicule. Phrases like 'You have no faith,' 'You are rebellious,' 'You are too young,' 'God's ways are not your ways,' and the biggies 'You are letting the devil use you,' and 'I am concerned about your soul.'

"Most of my questions surrounded 'free will,' 'a woman's place,' and a noticeable double standard that no one ever seemed to mention or care about. Here were these women working like dogs with fundraisers and committees, but never getting recognition, titles, power or promotions or, even better personal lives. It didn't seem fair, and I wanted to know why God required such sacrifice from women but not men?

"I also wanted to know why God sent some women husbands while others had been 'praying and waiting' a long time. Why didn't God just tell them 'no' if he wasn't going to give these faithful women what they wanted and the love they deserved? When this type of indoctrination starts so young and everyone reinforces such nonsense, a female child is doomed." ~ Mary L.

Oftentimes, the church social system sets women up to compete with each other over the scant few men in attendance, even those wholly unqualified for female attention. The church operates under the belief system that all men have a God-given right to have a female helper. (Genesis 2:18-22) *"Then the LORD God said, 'It is not good for the man to be alone; I will make him a helper suitable for him'."* Conveniently ignored are the many passages in the Bible that speak to a man being a wise person of understanding who follows the word of the Lord.

This is not meant to be a scriptural lesson; I am merely pointing out how Scriptures are used in black churches to bind women in a role of subservience to men. This mentality is part of the larger game of gaining control of your mind, and when that game is successfully won, the first prey trap snaps shut.

Church as the New Slave Master

> *"There is no development strategy more beneficial to society as a whole -- women and men alike -- than the one which involves women as central players."* ~Kofi Annan

With the female subservient thought process in effect, many women (most often single) are in the ministry "waiting to be found" and "working as unto the Lord" in the interim. This mindset leaves them vulnerable to abuse as the female church members are used as modern-day slaves by their pastors. The talents of women and men alike are used to build the church without any sort of compensation being offered for their efforts. The female congregants will get up early to help the pastor and the first family prepare for church, even cooking their meals and chauffeuring them to service. This dynamic is twisted and the roles reversed, because it is a pastor's role is to be a servant to his congregation, not theirs to be servants to him.

In one very large ministry there were several female members who were extremely good cooks, decorators and event planners. Their skills were discovered and they were subsequently given a "leadership" role in their church. They shopped, cooked, planned, cleaned and served visiting speakers. They were told that their gifts and talents would be put into an "account" (Phillipians 4:17) *Not that I desire your gifts; what I desire is that more be credited to your account.* This Scripture is often used to get women to do more and more for the church.

Those who read the entire Scripture realize it is part of a note of thanks to the people in a certain region who out of their abundance gave their money to Paul as he was out in another area talking to people about Christ. There is no bank in heaven that you can withdraw your good deeds from. In reality, when you work you deserve to get paid for your work whether the work is for business clients or your church. Your talents and job skills should bring in the hard-earned money you and your family deserve.

When we look at these examples of how Scripture is virtually held over the heads of many black women in the churches we can understand the "pimp" mentality of many of the male leaders. They are able to build a church of women willing to sacrifice time, talent and money with a promise that "GOD" will repay them at some future date.

Martyrdom and self-sacrifice is an important component of all Abrahamic religions, especially Christian and Muslim faiths. Women are especially prone to become martyrs to their church, as the belief that females are inferior and males superior is ingrained into the black woman's head almost from birth. Women are socialized to sacrifice and martyr themselves to their families ("a good mother puts her children before herself"), their spouses ("behind every successful man is a good woman"), their communities ("the backbone of the black community") and of course their pastors. The belief that a woman who suffers will be favored by God is most likely based upon 1 Peter 4:14-16: *"...Yet if anyone suffers as a Christian, let him not be ashamed, but let him glorify God in that name."*

Female members of the church will drive to "serve" with little to no gas in their cars, their families barely fed to do work in the house of God. These women are manipulated into believing that if they serve God, they will themselves be taken care of. Misquoted Scriptures and the willingness of black women to make God happy by some sort of penance keeps the women in these churches down and enslaved. The blind trust they give to the leaders in the church makes them easy targets for the psychological abuse derived from being taken advantage of. The Bible clearly teaches that a person cannot earn their way into God's good graces, nor is such sacrifice required.

"For by GRACE are ye saved through FAITH; and that not of yourselves: it is the GIFT of God: not of works, lest any man should boast."
(Ephesians 2:8-9)

Black women are taught (by pastors and black males in general) that she is inferior, unworthy, and must earn a man's favor by suffering. Part of the anguish means tolerating abusive, cold and dismissive behaviors from men in relationships which she "sacrifices" to save the marriage. Black women also believe that it is their burden to be of service to black men, sacrificing their bodies and self-respect to men by putting his well-being ahead of her own. Is it any wonder that black women are the most overweight and stressed demographic in the nation while they are simultaneously the most religious?

Many black women are extremely determined and will be seen "trying to make a dollar out of 15 cents" every day. During slavery black women learned to develop an extraordinary ability to survive situations and circumstances for years that would break a lesser woman in mere days. To stave off hunger, our ancestors scrounged and came up with creative ways to feed their families. What the slave owners threw away as scraps for the dogs (pig ears, pig feet, cow and pig intestines and ox tails), black women turned into delicacies that are now part of our cultural heritage and referred to as "soul food."

Black women are fond of the phrase "God don't put nothing on you that you can't handle" which would seem to equate a woman with a beast of burden, unquestioningly carrying the weight of the world on her shoulders. Accepting mistreatment and shouldering the responsibilities of others is a sure-fire way for the black woman to be preyed upon. Instead of accepting that it is her role to be prey, black women need to learn how to turn the tables on and best their predators.

Following and Worshipping Men, Not God

It is better to trust in the lord, than to put confidence in man! (Psalms 118:8)

It is imperative that African-American women stop being impressed by and blindly loyal to men period and black church leaders in particular. Every man should be properly vetted and not followed and freely trusted simply because of his gender or position. Just like the female members at New Life Baptist Church that looked foolish to the world for rallying around Bishop Eddie Long, you will soon get your face cracked when you put more faith in men than you do God.

> "There's drama in many churches, some just hide it better than others. The first church I went to with my family was chock full of nonsense. The pastor asked each member for a $1,000 donation toward rebuilding the church, and at the time, my mother was unable to give due to a divorce and financial problems. The pastor's wife gave my mom dirty looks every Sunday and stopped talking to her after she learned that my mom couldn't contribute. Now, I understand that pastors are supposed to receive a livable salary (and I'm sure many pastors have professions outside of church), but something is very wrong when your church is falling apart, heat not working, carpets torn up, but you live in a mansion with several luxury cars! I'm sure this is the case in many other churches as well, but not all. Needless to say, my mom thought the Lord was telling our family to worship elsewhere." ~ Tatiana K.

Pastors and ministers are not special, they are not unique, they are not anointed, and there is nothing about them that warrants being placed on a pedestal. Black women seem to forget that these guys are mere humans NOT GOD; they are just plain ol' men that burp and fart and get sick and bleed and lie and cheat and steal just like everyone else. The fact that they ARE mere men means that they often fall from grace and succumb to temptations of the flesh and greed like everyone else as well.

Being a pastor or minister is nothing but a job, a title, and has nothing to do with making that man better than any man on the street. This is one of the key reasons that women must stop glorifying and elevating church leaders to the status of perfect. They are not.

When egregious errors in judgment are pointed out to the faithful church-going sisters, their usual response is defensiveness and anger. Forever loyal to their pastors, these irate women will dismiss the accuser by saying that he or she is bitter and hates God. However, God has nothing to do with this foolishness! Neither does God have anything to do with the war against women and children being waged by twisted men in black churches. Church-going black women frequently mistake God and Jesus with a pastor, minister, or deacon. When someone is critical of your pastor and his behavior, it does not equate to criticizing God.

> "There is so much corruption in black churches, I've lost respect. If one must read the Bible it's best to do it at home and get your own spiritual understanding. I've known churches where the minister was stealing from the collection plate, where funds were embezzled and the

members all looked the other way as if nothing was happening. Yet this minister would get up in the pulpit on Sundays and preach as though he was holier than thou.

"Any woman who goes to church looking for spiritual guidance needs to find it within herself, first. She needs to first establish a healthy relationship with herself. Don't trust any man to give you what you are lacking from within and this includes religious men.

"And another important thing: black churches stay in folks' business too much. I've known couples who go to their church ministers with private matters for counseling, and the next thing you know, their business is all over the church. What kind of mess is that?" ~Glenda P.

She's made an excellent point. The power and influence the pastor seeks to maintain over his female church members is not limited to single women. If you notice, there aren't many married men that attend church services with their wives on a regular basis. It's because they want to eliminate opportunities for the pastor to stick his nose where it doesn't belong. Those men that go to church with their women often do so just to avoid an argument!

The Pastor in Your Marital Bed

Married men with wives in the church frequently complain that their woman puts her pastor, minister, bishop etc. on a pedestal, not her own husband. She comes in the door telling her husband what the pastor had to say – some other man – about what should happen with his household. That's infuriating and something black men are not trying to deal with.

Several men interviewed reported that their wife's insistent focus on what her pastor or minister had to say was the direct cause of their divorce. Their wife/partner listened to what some other man had to say about what he should do with his own money, in his house, with his children, and in his bedroom. These are private matters that should be discussed between the couple and no one else.

Most husbands would probably listen politely, as even black men that don't go to church still have respect for God and the man that represents God to his wife. He may even listen for a few months just to keep the peace. However, the women were so deeply ingrained in their religion and so enamored of their pastor that they just couldn't let it go.

So here you have a grown woman, married to a man that is providing for her and her children, who she sleeps next to every night putting some other man and what HE wants and says before her husband. How disrespected and unimportant do you think that would make a husband feel? How powerless would he feel in his own home, berated and told by his wife: "Pastor So and So thinks you don't know what you are doing, honey." Where does that demonstrate love, admiration and respect for the man you thought enough of to marry?

No matter how much you love your pastor, he is not your man – he is married to *his* wife. No matter how much you love your pastor, he runs nothing but his mouth when it comes to how your husband conducts his affairs in *his* home. No matter how much you love your pastor, he is not the father of your children and he pays nary a one of the bills in your home. No matter how much you love your pastor, he has no say-so about what goes on under your roof.

Pastor runs his house where he lives with *his wife*, and your husband runs the house where you live with *your husband*. You must NEVER confuse the roles of your husband and your pastor – they are two different entities with two completely different purposes and roles in your life. You must NEVER put some other man before your husband – it's the ultimate disrespectful act. If you want to do all that worshipping of your pastor, then don't get married.

3

MALE SAINTS AND FEMALE SINNERS

Slut-shaming and condemning female sexuality in the black church means sexual assaults, cheating and out-of-wedlock pregnancies are blamed
solely on women

One man cannot hold another man down in the ditch without remaining down in the ditch with him.
~Booker T. Washington (1856-1914)

Religious Judgments of Female Sexuality

All black men have been influenced in at least a small way by Christianity and its views on females and female sexuality. Church men are exceedingly judgmental about the female gender, and are some of the harshest critics of women and girls. Even black men who haven't set foot in a church in 30 years possess disparaging outlooks of female sexuality. However, negative judgments and condemnations of overtly sexual behavior apply to females only; never to themselves.

Men of the church seek to position themselves as leaders of the community, someone to be followed and admired by women, someone who holds himself separate and apart as better than other men. Yet, when it comes time to show strength of character, leadership and self-mastery they flip and present themselves as spineless jellyfish, totally controlled by their penises and base, animal instincts. They succumb to the biblical reference that all women are descendants of Eve the temptress. Just like any other unsaved man, pastors and ministers are led by their lusts of female flesh which means they are not special, not unique and nothing to glorify or follow anywhere.

"CHURCH MEN?! Church men be livin' dirty!!!!! When I was a strip club bartender, all kinds of men came through. Most often, the deacons and pastors and faithful were on their best behavior. However, more often than not, the very men who got kicked out for grabbing the dancers, or trying to make me serve them alcohol when they were already very drunk (that's illegal I could've lost my license), or trying to offer the dancers money for sex, were the 'good Christian brothers.' The bouncers even had jokes. They'd say, 'Go get that fool, he's trying to offer prayer services again.' Or, 'He wants to give whomever an exorcism' or, 'Brother Perv wants to lay hands on a sister!'" ~Denora M.

Women have been forced to bear the brunt of blame and responsibility for being coerced, assaulted or sexually harassed. If the victim speaks up and seeks justice for the crime, she is questioned and blamed for dressing in revealing clothing that "enticed" her assailant. The gossips in the church whisper, "You know how those types of women are!" If assaulted by a pastor or other high-level church official, the victim may also be accused of having a vendetta against the church, her true goal to bring down the ministry with shameful "lies." A church member attacked outside of church will be accused of being in the wrong place, eating or drinking something that she "shouldn't have" or questioned about what time of day she was wherever she was. Judgmental attitudes about female sexuality are part of the religious indoctrination where the Bible speaks of a woman's virtue, but never a man's. In the Bible, women are depicted as either virgin Madonnas, concubines of rich men or whores.

Even if a woman should have a consensual sexual relationship with her pastor, she is blamed exclusively for that as well. "You know a lot of gold-digging women go into church looking to get with a single pastor because they want to be the First Lady" the gossipy church members whisper. If the pastor is married and has an affair with a congregant, the Other Woman is blamed for "seducing" him and not being "a virtuous woman," -- as if the pastor were a mindless drone or puppet that had no choice in where he dropped his pants.

She Should Have Kept Her Legs Closed

"Ladies keep your virtue locked away for your husband. Stop spreading the wealth around (sex). I am married now for seven and a half years. I dated my wife for five years prior to marriage. WE NEVER had sex nor did we ever kiss – not once. Why? Because she set in her mind that she was not going to do that again until after she was married. Now this was hard for me until I met her, someone that meant what she said. What this will do for you is filter out the guys that are interested in one thing. Now if that is what you want then fine, stop complaining.

"Another very IMPORTANT piece this action added to our relationship was communication. With no sex, we had to fill in the gaps so we talked. A lot. We became very close and familiar with one another. I was blessed and so was my wife with the pleasure of marrying my best friend. Now three kids later we still have a very close relationship full of communication and lots of undefiled loving good sex. The way God planned it. Ladies, I beg you be patient and maintain your virtue." ~Robert T.

The dictionary defines virtue as: (1) the quality or practice of moral excellence or righteousness; (2) a particular moral excellence the virtue of tolerance; (3) (Christian Religious Writings / Theology) any of the cardinal virtues (prudence, justice, fortitude, and temperance) or theological virtues (faith, hope, and charity); (4) any admirable quality, feature, or trait; and (5) chastity, **esp in women** (emphasis mine)

Black men are frequently heard telling black women that they are too educated, too aggressive, too manly, too demanding and too picky. Black men enjoy telling black women that they need to be quiet, sit in the corner, listen to men and wait for a man to come pick her like a kitty in a pet-store window. Men in churches are constantly telling black women that if they pray hard enough, wait long enough, their prayers will be answered. Men are also telling women that they should keep their legs closed so that SHOULD a black man decide he might want to possibly consider marrying her, there won't be much mileage on her vagina.

In reality, a woman's vagina has nothing to do with her virtue. That type of judgmental thinking is a major part of the problem black men and women are having today. It's always wonderful to hear that a couple is happy and in love, raising their family together; it's great that he writes that he and his wife have found marital bliss.

However, it is curious that Robert T. assumed the success of his marriage is based upon the fact that his wife kept her legs locked and didn't have sex before marriage. If it took her withholding sex in order to make him learn to communicate with her, to make him learn how to show non-sexual affection, to make him have respect for her, and to make him put in the time to get to know her as a person, then the problem was never her…it was HIM!

> "I once had a Youth Leader/Pastor tell me that purity is only for girls. That meant to me that I didn't have to worry about any of that save-myself-for marriage stuff like my sister did." ~ Marcellus T.

The attitude expressed by Marcellus T. above is a CORE problem with Churchianity. It perverts women's perception of themselves and makes females feel like their only "virtue" is their vagina. It's a disgusting attitude and a very negative and judgmental mindset, deeply ingrained in black males. Due to the influence of religion on men's perception of females, black women are constantly told that all of our worth and humanity lie between our legs. Patriarchy mandates that women use the power between their legs (or NOT use it) as a bartering tool for a relationship. Women are essentially coerced into trading a lightly used vagina for respect, love and commitment from men.

Certainly, women should exercise sexual discernment, but only as meets their own standards and solely for themselves. Guilt tripping and slut-shaming are two of the primary ways in which religion steals women's power - by making us feel like our bodies and our sexuality aren't owned by us, but instead are "gifts" to be saved and given to men.

Women can refuse to tolerate male attempts to control and suppress female sexuality as the "right" way to be. Ownership of your own body means that you do not "hold out" for the highest bidder, whether he is bidding financially, emotionally or with personal validation (*i.e.* putting a ring on it). You owe no one your "virtue" but yourself. Many women are devastated when they find out that holding out, playing coy, following ALL the rules men established to measure female sexuality doesn't work anyway.

Being virtuous before marriage didn't stop her husband from cheating after the novelty of having a virgin bride wore off. Being virtuous didn't stop her husband from withholding affection, from being physically or emotionally abusive. Being virtuous didn't stop her husband from being sexually selfish, inconsiderate, from fathering children outside the marriage or simply not loving and cherishing her the way she was made to believe he would if she "kept her virtue" and "her purity." Not having the sex you want to have should never be a ploy to garner respect from men or a ring.

She Tried to Trap Him!

Single black women with more than one child born out of wedlock are condemned within the black church. This is especially true if the woman involved has two or more children by two or more different fathers. Yet, the single men that have multiple "baby mommas" and three or four children borne out of wedlock are excused from culpability. "Those women were trying to trap him!" the church mothers say as they rally to the male's defense. "Those heffas should have used birth control or kept their legs closed" are the snidely whispered comments. "More than 70 percent of black children are born to single mothers – what are these girls doing?" say the old biddies as they shake their head in disgust.

Black men both in and out of church have no problem succumbing to their lust by sleeping with a woman then absolving themselves of any responsibility connected with that sex act. One of their favorite responsibility-avoidance tactics is to refuse to wear a condom when having sex. When the woman they slept with becomes pregnant, they get angry at HER for "making me become a father when I didn't want to be one!" Never mind that he knew how children are created and performed the acts that guarantee that a child is conceived. He conveniently twists reality to make the irresponsible handling of his seed the sole fault of the female.

Other black women assist in perpetuating this fraud by excusing and defending men by declaring that "it wasn't his fault" or "she's lying, that's not his baby!" -- as if they were eyewitnesses to the events that created the child. Mothers of sons are the worst in this regard. For some reason, refusing to accept the fact that if their son slept with the woman in question even once, there is at least a 50 percent chance that the baby they are denying is indeed their grandchild.

And when it's pointed out that he was wrong for fornicating or committing adultery in the first place, these male-identified women and defensive men inevitably fall back to the standard woman-shaming rhetoric, "Well, she should have kept her legs closed!" Though he whined, begged and tried every trick in the book (sometimes for months) to get them open, the fact that he voluntarily placed himself between said legs is dismissed as an irrelevant point. It's all HER fault that this happened. He and his band of defensive supporters may go so far as to accuse her of having slept with half the neighborhood, which is, in their minds, why the baby can't possibly be his -- though she wasn't any of those things when he was trying to have sex with her.

The finger-pointing and blaming expresses his true mindset – he expected to lay down, experience sexual pleasure and get up having suffered no repercussions. He refuses to accept responsibility or acknowledge that there is indeed a price to pay for his actions. The women blame her by saying she should have used birth control or "made him" use a condom. The involved female is labeled a trifling bitch or a nasty whore, and sometimes both.

I've also heard of several incidents involving teenaged girls impregnated by someone they were led to believe loved them, most often an older male who coerced the teen to have sex with him. In several other cases, the pregnancy was the result of child molestation/rape. I was horrified to hear that young girls around the country have been ordered to stand up in front of their congregations and profess their "sins." The pregnant female was shamed and humiliated, whereas once again, the male that made the pregnancy possible gets off the hook with his reputation unscathed. It's a horrible double standard damaging to the psyche of the pregnant female.

Even more ridiculous is the fact that the single women in the church will view a two- or three-time "baby daddy" as a viable candidate for a husband. In spite of the fact that the women have living proof these types of men place no value on commitment, he will get lots and lots of female attention.

Why do church women excuse black men for doing the same things that black women do, without requiring them to suffer any consequences? Why is it that a woman with three baby daddies is nothing but a hood rat or a slut, but a man with three baby mamas is socially acceptable to women in church? This is another sexist double standard common in black church society that makes absolutely no sense.

Enslavement of Women through Child Bearing

African Americans are the most religious and God-fearing race of people in the nation, yet we have the highest number of children born out of wedlock, the highest number of children being raised in single-parent homes, the highest rate of poverty among children and the highest rate of new HIV/AIDS cases. We also have the highest rates of children in the foster care system, in special-needs classes and in the nation's prisons. I believe that the vast majority of these social issues are directly tied to beliefs that originate in the black church.

Young females are set up to become pregnant single mothers due to a series of mixed messages and gender-based double standards perpetuated by church leaders and members. Though the concept that women should be kept barefoot and pregnant is one of the most sexist ever created, the reality is that black churches encourage and support the single-mother lifestyle which keeps women in emotionally weakened, psychologically subservient, economically dependent positions to men. Once a young woman becomes pregnant, her goals are pushed aside and her dreams deferred as she takes on the responsibilities of motherhood all alone.

- **Lack of Sex Education for Girls Leads to Teen Pregnancies.** The religious community's focus on "abstinence only" sex education does teens a great disservice by keeping them ignorant about their reproductive systems. Besides being told not to have sex (*i.e.,* "keep your dress down and your legs closed!"), no real information about female sexuality and birth control is provided to young black females from their church-going parents. There seems to be a common belief that providing daughters with birth control and sexual reproduction information encourages them to go out and have sex, when in reality the opposite is true. Several studies have shown a clear correlation between religious beliefs and a high teen pregnancy and out-of-wedlock birth rate. Other studies show that states that stress "abstinence-only" sex education rank the highest in the numbers of underage pregnancies. However New York, New Jersey and California have mandated comprehensive sex education and these states reflect the lowest pregnancy rates for minority teens. In our modern society no female child should be unaware of the games men play using words of love to get sex, or how to protect herself from unwanted pregnancy. Lack of solid information or use of birth control options means that many young women have no female health examinations, pap smears, or breast cancer screenings, nor do they know how to protect themselves from STDs should they decide to have sex.

- **Glorification of Single Motherhood.** The vicious cycle of single motherhood is generational and, unfortunately, normalized in the black community. It is quite possible for a black woman to be a grandmother when she is only 30 years of age – she had her baby at age14 or 15, and her daughter had HER baby at age 14 or 15 as well. If everyone around has the same family makeup, how could you know any better? With 75 percent of the children in the black community born into single-parent, mother-headed households, a void is created in the lives of millions of women and children educationally, emotionally and financially. Though a pregnant teen will hear "a baby is a blessing" from church members, the reality is that being a single teen mother is no joke and it makes life much harder than it needs to be. A young woman that has yet to establish herself and has no resources to provide for a child will struggle with exhaustion and unnecessary stress. It will also take her years to meet goals that are about actualizing dreams of greatness, instead of focusing on meeting immediate survival needs.

- **You Can't Kill Your Baby!** Most church members are against abortions, with men (surprisingly) being some of the staunchest advocates of a woman having a child even if the father is nowhere in the picture. Others will suggest that the girl have the baby and give it up for adoption versus have an abortion. In reality black children are not adopted; instead they languish in foster homes until they are 18 when they are booted out on the street. In either case, the girl is told "don't kill your baby!" She is encouraged to use her body to birth the child of a man that has no interest in her or the child to secure the approval of other people. In light of the drastic changes becoming a mother will have on the life of a young unmarried woman, abortion is a legal and viable option for her to utilize. No girl should be made to feel guilt or shame if she chooses to have an abortion. Perhaps she wants to finish high school and go to college. Maybe she doesn't want to carry a baby to full term and give it up for an adoption; she just wants her life back right now. Guilt-tripping a young woman into having a child she is ill-equipped to care for is one of the quickest ways to clip her wings and make sure she stays down for a decade if not longer. She will also stay in church praying for the strength to make it through.

- **Don't Worry, God Will Make a Way!** This overused phrase is said to young women that find themselves accidentally pregnant. Others, usually single mothers or baby-daddy's themselves, will do all they can to try to convince her not to have an abortion, and join their struggling ranks. Many of the church members are self-serving and single-mindedly focus on the unborn fetus instead of the burden and responsibilities that will be placed on a young flower that hasn't yet had the opportunity to bloom. An out-of-wedlock pregnancy should never be romanticized, but instead addressed with a firm dose of reality. Young females must understand that the chief responsibility for the pregnancy and all the blame for it will fall on their shoulders. The GIRL gets told she should have kept her legs closed. The GIRL gets stuck with the day-to-day care of the baby. The GIRL has to drop out of school to care for her child. The GIRL gets stuck at some minimum wage job for 10 years while she tries to finish school -- if she can even get that kind of support. The GIRL gets tied down and can't have fun like a teen should. The GIRL gets told "God will make a way" while she is broke and can't even buy diapers for the baby. When a baby is born, all of the change and the great impact are on the life of female. While she battles fatigue and poverty, the male sperm donor is off doing his thing, finishing school and making his way in the world as if nothing happened. Again, another way for the young woman to be tied down and her wings clipped.

- **Men Don't Want a Ready-Made Family.** Statistics show that teen mothers are more likely to drop out of school, live in poverty and remain unmarried than women that do not have children out of wedlock. The romantic market is already challenging even for a single black woman that has herself together! So when a young woman drags along the baggage of children into a new relationship, she creates even more of a barrier to a walk down the aisle. Most unmarried young men with no children feel as Kirk (24) does: "I don't want a ready-made family. They may be perfectly wonderful children, but they aren't mine. I want to spend my time, money and love raising my own children. It also doesn't help that they are a constant living reminder of her life before me - specifically, of another man sleeping with her, and her caring about him enough to carry his children." Chet is a bit older (42) and has tried dating single moms without much luck: "I tried it… was an awful hassle just trying to get to know them. You start of second or third to the kids, their real dad, her crazy schedule. This means plans revolve around the kids and their schedule, not just yours and hers, and that makes it extra difficult to schedule anything. That romantic dinner, sitter canceled, is now at Chuck E. Cheese. That weekend get away… impossible. You have to win her over and win the kids over, which makes it twice as much work. It's damn near impossible since many don't let you even meet the kids for a while. Her attitude is often: If it does 'work out' they will be her kids, you will just be that wallet, I mean the guy that she allows to babysit them. Equal parent, forget that!"

The problem is compounded if the baby-daddy is a trouble-maker and does all he can to bring the drama. Most men would rather not be bothered, so they find a woman without children to marry.

Adult females need to be honest and tell young women any and every time to fulfill their dreams and potential before considering a baby. The risks are high for both the mother and the child. Children of teen mothers are more likely to be born at low birth weight, grow up poor, live in single-parent households, experience sexual abuse and neglect, and to enter the child welfare system. Daughters of teen mothers are statistically 22 percent more likely to become teen parents themselves. Children of teen mothers do worse in school: they are 50 percent more likely to fail a grade, more likely to drop out of high school, and have lower scores on standardized achievement tests. Sons of teen mothers are also 13 percent more likely to end up in prison.

There is also an obvious parallel that church folks choose to conveniently overlook: If there is a single mother, there is a single father as well. Not one child on this planet has been born without the participation of a male. To create a human life requires a fertile ovum from a female and sperm from a male; even children conceived in test tubes and laboratories are formed from those two key ingredients. Excusing men from their responsibility in creating pregnancies is harmful to both females and children. By attempting to manipulate, guilt trip or coerce young women to have babies out of wedlock, the church women assist men in preying on the emotional insecurities of females and their offspring.

No young women should ever change or forego her dreams for a man, especially since one who truly loves her wouldn't want her to anyway. Self protect by waiting to have children until you are a mature, stable adult. Self protect by picking the right man to father your children – one that understands the value of love and who holds family in high regard. Self protect by completing your education past high school which opens up thousands of career opportunities. Self protect by having your own best interest at the forefront of EVERYTHING you do, because being a single parent is in no one's best interest.

Young women must learn that sex is not a toy, nor is it a gift to "give" a man in an attempt to get love. Most times you'll be left with two things you really didn't want - a baby and a broken heart.

Single Black Women as Jezebels

"Nature says women are human beings, men have made religions to deny it. Nature says women are human beings, men cry out no!" ~ Taslima Nasrin

The Jezebel Spirit is a popular term used to further confine women to subservient roles of service to men in black churches. This is nothing new, as the control and manipulation games of black churches have been in place for generations. The words and methodology have changed slightly for 21st century audiences, but the outcomes for women are similar.

Women in black churches are taught to obey men from an early age. Should a woman question church leadership or male authority, she is deemed to have a Jezebel Spirit. According to the Bible, "Jezebel was the daughter of Ethbaal, King of the Phoenicians, and one of the wives of Ahab, King of North Israel. Her story is recounted in 1 Kings and 2 Kings, where she is described as a worshiper of the god Baal and the goddess Asherah, and as an enemy of God's prophets." (About.Com)

Being labeled as having a Jezebel Spirit is a very negative thing in the black church. A Jezebel is considered to be cunning, manipulative, a sexual deviant and someone to be ostracized and ignored. This, in the black church, is like putting someone in solitary confinement. A woman that asks questions about biblical doctrine or practices is told to keep quiet and not challenge the work or word of God, as she has allowed a spirit of Jezebel to overtake her. These women are often used as scapegoats and examples of what happens when or if you question authority. Use of this psychological mind game is similar to the scare tactics used by street pimps who will slap one of their 'ho's in front of the other girls as a demonstration of his power. Beating someone physically or verbally serves as a threat that if you act in similar ways the crap will be slapped out of you too.

> "At the last church I was a member of in Texas, the pastor's wife got up one Sunday toward the end of service and said that the women needed to present themselves better in the church because a lot of new men were coming to the church and had told her and her husband that they were 'hittin' it' in the first week of meeting a woman at the church. I was livid. I went to her after church and asked did she check the clowns that had said that to her? Were they coming into the church seducing women perhaps? Instead of always blaming the women (since it really does take two to tango), shouldn't the men be held responsible for their actions as well? The message of the church overall is to 'blame' women for any sex at all." ~Gabrielle T.

Black men operating under the influence of patriarchal belief systems supported by church doctrine tend to focus a lot of their energy on negating women, always pointing out the physically attractive, well built, young woman that stirs his loins, while simultaneously referring to her as a Jezebel or harlot. If she is now or has been sexually active in the past, she is really in trouble.

Lust and the Virtuous Woman

Throughout history men (whether Christian or not) have struggled with their lust. Any man who denies that he does is either lying due to his fear of being seen as weak, lying to manipulate a woman, lying out of embarrassment, or a combination of all three. In the minds of the deeply religious, men are perfect and innocent, and only enticed to cheat on their wives, rape women or molest children because someone outside themselves 'made' them do it. A favored tactic is to assign responsibility for their feelings of sexual excitement to women/Satan, rather than to openly acknowledge and take full responsibility for their own spiritual weakness and inability to control their thoughts and actions.

Since these men are aware of the fact that they cannot control their own thoughts, they are suspicious that other men cannot control theirs either. They don't want other men having lust-filled sexual thoughts about their daughters and wives. To keep other males in check, men concocted a ridiculous set of rules and regulations to which women must adhere in order to escape men's harsh judgments and ridicule.

I addressed this issue in a piece entitled "The Male Struggle to Control Female Sexuality", which was written in response to a letter from a male reader, who claimed sexually active women lower their implicit value:

> "Your view of women ensures that young females will continue to view themselves as people defined only in relation to their body. These impressionable young women will continue to feel insecure about their looks, and will always seek male approval about their bodies. Most will believe that their value as a good and worthy person is totally dependent on toeing the line and behaving in ways that men list as approved sexual behaviors for females. I really wonder who you guys think you are and why you believe you have the right to dictate and regulate what women do with their own body.
>
> "As if your shaming and berating women who enjoy sex weren't enough, in our society, sex and sexuality are also legally regulated. The roots of these laws are found in the religious (Christian) based origin of this country ("in God We Trust"). For centuries, both in Europe and the U.S., Christianity has used the words of the Bible to suppress sexuality and control it. I've stated repeatedly that in my opinion, organized religion was created strictly to place men in a dominant position over women, in order to control what women wear, say, can do out in the world, and do with their genitals.
>
> "Men are encouraged to 'sow their wild oats' and to remember that there are 'plenty of fish in the sea' so they should 'not settle down too quickly.' The more young

women he sullies, the more his male relatives and friends gaze upon him with manly pride.

"However, if a woman of the same age and social rank has sex with even a moderate number of men, she is looked down upon, called a nasty whore, a skank, or a skeezer, and her 'value' as a potential mate is reduced. As a matter of fact, laws had to be enacted to protect rape victims from being vilified in courts for being sexually active. Defense attorneys would try to use a woman's history of sexual activity against her, thus providing a built-in excuse for the rapist… the general attitude of these men being 'well, she wasn't a virgin anyway, so what difference does it make that she got raped?'

"Sandwiching women's sexuality even further between male camps of disapproval and judgment is the fact that men are constantly being brought up on charges for sexual harassment of women, in violation of the very laws other men created to protect women's virtue.

"Men even went so far as to use religion as justification to lock women into metal chastity belts to reduce the opportunity to engage in premarital sex. This act of cruelty represents male dominance at its worst. With the aid of a lock and key, a male asserted total control over the female's genitals, and thus removed her ability to decide what she does with her own pussy."

Under the cloud of patriarchy and religion, women must effectively take charge not only of their own sexuality, but that of multitudes of strange men. To avoid being shamed by the men and women of their church for standing out or being considered sexy, a woman must always be on guard about how she MIGHT be coming across, blaming herself for how men approach her. In the black church, women are assigned responsibility for monitoring their behavior, language and attire in order to be considered a virtuous woman. I believe this twisted mentality is one of the reasons why modesty and lack of "adornments" is heavily emphasized in most religions for women.

Fundamentalist Mormon sects insist that their women wear long shapeless granny dresses that cover their bodies from neck to toe (though a long dress can be lifted just as quickly as a short one). In some Islamic countries, women wear a burqa – a dark cloak that covers everything but their eyes. And in African-American Church of God in Christ (COGIC) churches, women are forbidden to wear makeup, jewelry or do much to fix themselves up. The following text is from the Official Handbook for Department of Women, Church of God in Christ, Inc.:

> "We close by admonishing our young women and girls to let your manner and your clothing reflect the Jesus that you sing and testify about. The world is looking for an example, a model, why not be that one? Most of all make certain that your hearts are right with the Lord, for it is the 'hidden man of the heart.' (I Peter 3:3)

> "Holy Women are asked to refrain from make-up, such as eye shadow, lipstick, colored fingernail polish, etc.

"Holy women should be careful of accepting the latest fashions, because some of them do not represent modesty in dress.

"Pants are not included in the dress code for Holy women."

By preaching messages of female chastity, virtue and responsibility for inciting men's lust, men of the church have effectively excused themselves from being mature adults that control what they do and how they do it. By burdening women with the responsibility for controlling men's thoughts and behavior through her actions, attire, words and location, men of the church have let themselves off the hook. This is just another facet of the con game of Churchianity.

"This is why I was always skeptical of the so-called church men. Honestly, some of them are no better than the street thugs. And since they claim themselves to be men of God, why the hell they worried about so-called hookers or ungodly women, and why the hell are men of God calling women out of their names? Why not instruct your fellow godly men to stop looking for so-called hookers and prostitutes on Facebook? Damn some black men don't have shit else to do but blame black women for everything! Go deal with important issues like fatherless homes, people with drug addictions and why so many black men are killing each other. Dickheads are not trying to put other men in check. That would mean they would have to put themselves in check. It's so obvious even Stevie Wonder can see it. Don't nobody wanna

75

constantly read or hear shit from these men about what women are doing wrong!" ~Ebony Q.

I've been told repeatedly by men that I'm wrong to lead women to think more about themselves, and that I should be telling women to think more about men because men think about women all the time. I believe that to be true – men do think about women quite a bit.

The problem is WHAT men think about women. A lot of black men don't think about women as people with their own minds, hearts and bodies. Black men, especially those indoctrinated in the church mindset of male supremacy, don't think about what women care about, what makes women happy, what women dream of, their life goals, nor their pains. All men with a sexist mindset think about women is how to get from us what they want with as little risk to themselves as possible, and how to make women do what they want them to do. Use of religion as funneled through black churches is most often the weapon of choice.

4

PRAY, PAY AND OBEY!

Dominating and controlling females psychologically, emotionally and financially by any means necessary

I freed a thousand slaves. I could have freed a thousand more if only they knew they were slaves.~ Harriet Tubman (1820-1913)

Black Women: The Most Religious Demographic in the U.S.

> *All religions are founded on the fear of the many and the cleverness of the few*
> ~Stendhal (1783-1842)

Black females have long been considered the backbone of the black community and the cornerstone of their families and churches. But what is the real price Black women have paid to wear this crown of fool's gold?

An examination of any congregation of the average black church shows that single black females fill the pews. Results of a recent study "African-Americans and Religion" by the PEW Research Center's Forum on Religion and Public Life found that "African-Americans are markedly more religious on a variety of measures than the U.S. population as a whole."

According to the survey, almost 90 percent of African-Americans express "absolutely certain belief in God" compared to just over 70 percent of the total U.S. population. Two other important statistics gleaned from this survey: (1) 80 percent of black Americans report that religion is "very important" in their lives, compared to 57 percent of the general U.S. population; and (2) 55 percent of black Americans report that they "interpret Scripture literally" compared to 32 percent of the general U.S. population.

The PEW study also reported that "Men are significantly more likely than women to claim no religious affiliation. Nearly one in five men say they have no formal religious affiliation, compared with roughly 13 percent of women."

The survey shows a distinct correlation between religion and social attitudes amongst African Americans. "African Americans who are more religiously observant (as defined by frequency of worship service attendance and the importance of religion in their lives) are more likely to oppose abortion and homosexuality, and more likely to report higher levels of conservative ideology." Female submission is a very popular concept among black males.

Christians and Female Submission

> *Find out just what any people will quietly submit to and you have the exact measure of the injustice and wrong which will be imposed on them.*
> ~ Frederick Douglass (1818-1895)

Church-going women are socialized to be submissive to men, and are thoroughly trained to do so with Biblical Scriptures. The view that women are inferior to men has become a key component in the lies and games used to subjugate black women in churches by black pastors. The Old Testament's decree of male supremacy (I Cor. 11:3, 8-9) has kept woman inferior to man for centuries. In the black church and most religions, the default human is one with a penis, and only men receive respect or power within the church.

Though the Old Testament has many passages that portray women as nothing but evil, commodities and slaves to their husbands, it also contains many contradictory messages. I do not believe that God's purpose was to create women as an inferior beings. After all, women are referred to as "the glory of man" (1 Cor. 11:7) by God who also instructed men to honor, take care of and protect their wives as delicate beings and partners (1 Peter 3:7; Eph 5:25, 5:28, 5:33; Col. 3:19). That means women are to be respected, revered, loved completely and with honesty, and put on a pedestal.

Typically, black men looking for Scripture to back up their self-serving beliefs quickly point to Genesis 2:18, where God creates a "helpmeet" for Adam and Genesis 3:16, where a woman is instructed to allow a man to rule over her. "Look! It's right here in the Bible!" they say. "All helpers are subordinate to the ones they help, which proves women are here to serve men." This amazing leap in logic totally (and conveniently) ignores Psalms (10:14, 27:9, and118:7), where God is praised as man's helper. Even black men who are not in church, and who have no thoughts of an engagement or marriage in their heads, will hit a woman with the "God says you need to submit to me because I'm a man!" routine. Many women fall right in line instead of reminding him that the command to submit is two-fold and that God said husband only, not boyfriend or baby daddy.

Anyway, how can female obedience and submissiveness be justified when women are the source of the power fueling every black church in the nation? Black men do not give their money to other black men to help support their lifestyle or sex life! If even just half of the female congregants stopped giving money to black churches this week, within a month 75 percent of black churches would be perilously close to bankruptcy. Black women have an amazing amount of power that they are for some reason hesitant to wield.

> "We were told that a woman should work all week, then give her entire check to her husband because the Bible said so. WTF? In Bible study I saw one husband pressure his wife to do this. If it was me, I would have

quit my job, since the Bible says the husband is supposed to take care of the household and everything in it. Don't know what happened to them. Didn't see them in Bible study anymore after that." ~Tabitha C.

Female members of every congregation support the church with monetary donations, and by organizing fundraising and social events. It is the women of the church that volunteer their time to cook, clean, and provide assistance to the males with the titles and true power. Though women lead committees and are very influential in their churches, few black women are in a real position of power as the spiritual leader of their own churches.

This subservient mentality also includes actually finding relationships that grow her own purpose. She is frequently directed to have the men of the church and a male in her life "check out" the possible suitor she has, as these men demand the right to determine if a woman and man are "equally yoked." This mandate positions grown men and women as subservient children, requiring that they "ask" the pastor for permission to date. Is this not a cult-like mentality, with the pastor having placed himself in the role of Decider of all Things… a God? Women believe they must obey these requests to be worthy in the eyes of the Lord. They refuse to listen to the advice of people outside the church deeming them "not having the MIND OF CHRIST," another buzz phrase used to make submission palatable.

> "The Bible teaches that woman brought sin and death into the world, that she precipitated the fall of the race, that she was arraigned before the judgment seat of Heaven, tried, condemned and sentenced. Marriage for

her was to be a condition of bondage, maternity a period suffering and anguish, and in silence and subjection, she was to play the role of a dependent on man's bounty for all her material wants, and for all the information she might desire... Here is the Bible position of woman briefly summed up." ~Elizabeth Cady Stanton (1815-1902)

Traditional Jewish men, at the beginning of the daily morning prayers say: *"Blessed are you, Lord, our God, ruler the universe who has not created me a woman."* Laws in effect at the time the Bible was written deemed that a woman was not a person, but a thing. She could be killed, but not murdered. She had no legal rights whatsoever and no voice; she was absolutely her husband's possession to do with as he wished. Though there are Scriptures which show Jesus bucked many of the rigid rules about females and propriety, Bible-based attitudes of female inferiority continue to impact treatment of women in African-American churches to this day.

The concept of female submission is very dangerous to black women. Men feel entitled by biblical Scriptures to demean, degrade and use women in any way they please. When a woman feels defeated, weak and insignificant, she also feels helpless -- incapable of defending either herself or her children lest she go against the word of God. When a woman turns over her power to a man, his quest for even greater dominance may result in his use of the Bible to justify emotional, verbal or physical abuse.

Domestic Violence and the Church

Several years ago author Denise George released a book entitled *What Women Wish Pastors Knew*. She cites a survey in which nearly 6,000 pastors were asked how they would counsel women who came to them for help with domestic violence. Twenty-six percent admitted that they would advise a woman to continue to "submit" to her husband, no matter what. Twenty-five percent said they told wives the abuse was their own fault—for failing to submit in the first place. Astonishingly, 50 percent of the clergymen said women should be willing to "tolerate some level of violence" because it is better than divorce. Advice like this, Ms. George warns, often puts women "in grave danger".

Another study of 350 battered women found that 28 percent of them had sought advice from their clergyman (Pagelow, 1981b, pp. 277-300). In this study, the top responses the women received were (a) a reminder of their wifely duty accompanied by instructions to forgive and forget; (b) referral to another resource to limit church involvement; and (c) useless advice based strictly on religious doctrine that was not only insensitive to the women's needs for help, but at times, both asinine and dangerous. How is being ordered to pray more going to help prevent a woman from being verbally or emotionally crushed by a man that claims to love her? How is being reminded of your vows "for better or worse," going to prevent a husband from beating you half to death? "One, scolded by her minister for 'betraying' her husband by revealing what had occurred in the privacy of their home, was beaten harder by her husband when the pastors told him of her visit" (Pagelow & Johnson, 1988, p. 5).

Though everyone is familiar with the bruises, broken bones and scars associated with physical abuse, the most common types of abuse suffered by black women are verbal and emotional abuse. Emotional abuse is the least recognized type of abuse, probably because it is so common in black culture, tainting nearly all communications between black men and women.

A widely-held belief among black men is that a woman is to blame if she has a relationship with an abusive man, as she should have "picked" better. It is interesting to me how few black men ever demand that a male take responsibility for abusing females. Shifting blame from the attacker to the victim makes these men as emotionally abusive as the men they are so anxious to absolve of guilt. Black women are just as bad, instead focusing on why the abused female didn't leave rather than why he would abuse a woman in the first place.

When a woman is in an abusive relationship, the verbal abuser attacks his partner's character and the very essence of who she is as a person. His communications are insulting, critical, devaluing and mocking. Everything he says is constructed to undermine her sense of worth. Sadly, most women in emotionally abusive relationships have learned to deal with the hurt by ignoring their man's psychological assaults just to "keep the peace."

Emotional abuse is largely misunderstood as it leaves no visible wounds; instead, the emotionally abusive man batters and bruises his woman's self-esteem and confidence. Sarcastic comments, humiliation, blaming, trivializing, being overly demanding of a woman's time and energy, and "jokes" at her expense are all common ways emotional abusers wield their weapons and wage war on women. Repeatedly pointing out your perceived flaws, withholding affection, information and sex, and denying the reality of your feelings, thoughts and opinions are key ways he attacks.

The abuser believes he must always have influence over women and superiority in his household and relationship; these beliefs are reinforced by religion. The Book of Genesis has been used by such men to justify aggression toward and abuse of women: *"in sorrow thou shalt bring forth children: and thy desire shall be to thy husband, and he shall rule over the"*. And in Eph. 5:22-24 *"Wives, be subject to your own husbands, as to the Lord. For the husband is the head of the wife, as Christ also is the head of the church, He Himself being the Savior of the body. But as the church is subject to Christ, so also the wives ought to be to their husbands in everything."* Just as white slave master did to their slaves, black men use the Scriptures to justify their position of enslavement and dominance of women.

Religious doctrine also sets a woman up to believe that she is solely responsible for the health and happiness of her relationship and partner. The female is beaten over the head with guilt and brainwashed into believing that she has to work harder, give more and be a better woman to gain his approval. She feels it's her responsibility to improve the relationship all by herself. The abuser reinforces a twisted perception of reality by quoting Scriptures and telling her that she is not a "good Christian woman" that "submits to her man" if she doesn't perform to his standards.

I believe it is fair to say that the vast majority of black men are now or have at some point behaved in a fashion that qualifies as emotionally abusive to women. Black men as a whole treat women as less important than themselves, an attitude exacerbated by church doctrine. Women must not be deceived by outward trappings of success and think that a man that looks like he is about something cannot be abusive and sexist. Abusers wear no warning label. Even so-called "good" black men – highly educated and successful -- can be emotionally, verbally or physically abusive.

Single black women are instructed to seek a church-going man, a God-fearing man, a man that places love of the Lord first in his life. In the black church, women receive the clear message that they will not be fulfilled in their role as a woman if they are not married with children, period. It would follow then, that a married woman might stay in an abusive relationship longer than she should, due to her fear that leaving would make her somehow lose favor with God or face in church for abandoning her husband and marriage.

Of course a single woman has to first find this God-fearing, church going husband, who is about as mythical as a unicorn in the average black church.

5

THE SINGLE BLACK WOMAN IN CHURCH

Twisted courtship rituals have created several generations of black women terrified to ask for what they need or want in romantic relationships, so they settle for whatever they can get

Whatever you fear most has no power - it is your fear that has the power. ~Oprah Winfrey

Games of Love and Romance Played on Single Women

Black women have gotten to the point where they believe they must "prove" to their potential black male suitors that their love "don't cost a thing." Black women around the country will bend over backward to give to and support a man of God that "needs a little help," as they work to prove to him what a great wife they would be. Suffering and emotional pain, being dogged out and forgiving is viewed as part and parcel of the romantic equation.

There are also men that will use your emotional need for trust to take the heat off their own negative behaviors. Gaslighting is a tool often used by patriarchal men to make a woman believe something that isn't true or never happened. Gaslighting is a mind game abusive men use to distract women from their own problematic behaviors and to create self-doubt in their female target. The woman is left in a state of confusion, wondering why she can't remember the events he so convincingly describes. Many men can be very persuasive liars, especially to a woman that loves him and wants to believe in him.

Gaslighting is used to make a woman more emotional and therefore more needy, dependent and controllable. Black women have been gaslighted for decades, and in 2012 are afraid of demanding that a man take them out on dates, pay for the date, court them, or show an interest other than sexual. Somehow, the fact that every other race of women in the world requires their man to be financially solvent and to demonstrate gentlemanly courting behaviors is ignored. Black women have been tricked into believing that black females should not expect to be treated in such a manner because they don't deserve it.

The rituals of courtship have been flipped, with black men playing the role of the pursued and black women the pursuers. Black women expend an amazing amount of energy trying to figure out a way to convince a broke, needy, irresponsible man to wife her up. Desperate and lonely, many black women will pay out the nose with money and eventually their self respect, taking care of low-quality suitors that they find in church.

The inevitable outcome of such games is that millions of black women who want very much to be married go home year after year alone. Millions of black females spend the best years of their reproductive and sexual lives in lonely frustration on their knees praying for something that will never come because black men of strength do not go to church. And instead of doing what is needed to bring more men of quality into churches, or providing women with the tools to go out into the world and find what they want themselves, single church women are told that "God will bring you your husband" and "he must be equally yoked" or some such nonsense – all ludicrous and contradictory mind games.

Other messages single women are getting are to stay hidden and allow their husband to find them, to pray and live a righteous and chaste life, and that they must give to the church to receive blessings from God. Millions of unmarried black women are being told by their pastors that according to the word of God, these are the steps required and how a woman is supposed to behave and dress in order for Jesus to bless her with both a husband and abundance.

Let's start with that "stay hidden so someone can find you" thing.

I recall a few years back when all the police and spies in the world couldn't find Osama Bin Laden. Teamster organizer Jimmy Hoffa disappeared in 1975 and with every FBI agent and police officer in the nation searching, we STILL can't find him! But one man searching through millions of women is supposed to find you? What flavor of fool would I have to be to believe that?

It is to the pastor's advantage that you stay hidden in his church. As a good Christian single woman, you tithe to your church home and support special projects with even more of your hard-earned cash. While there, he feeds your fantasies of happily ever after, and you fill his pockets with Benjamins. He fuels dreams that you will finally have someone to love, and you fill his pockets with dead presidents. He does everything he can to keep single men out of the church and away from the women under his control, while you fill his pockets with cold hard cash. Instructing women to stay hidden is all part of the game to keep you in church so that you can continue giving the Pastor and his church your time and money.

> "I remember being a member of a church that had one single guy in it – one. All of the women were all over this guy. Trying to take him to lunch, babysit his daughter. It was crazy. And every Sunday the pastor was laying hands and telling us our man was going to come through the door. Really? There is one single guy here… 100 women and one single man. How is that possibly going to happen? Why am I looking for my husband here? There has to be other places to meet men. Do I have to meet him at this particular church? And the response was 'yes, you need to meet him here because we

need to make sure he was being taught by us and has the right beliefs.'" ~Marilyn S.

This game has been played on women for decades and is nothing new. A sad story of a beautiful young woman's life wasted waiting on the man that her pastor said she should wait for was shared with me recently. This woman's story about her grandmother began back in the 1950s when her grandmother was a 20-something year-old widow:

> "I was in my mid-teens when I figured out the scam that has been perpetuated by black churches for eons. I watched my beloved maternal grandmother who had been widowed at a very young age waste her entire life waiting for that magical Christian black man who was going to embody all the things her preacher droned on and on about week after week, year after year. But all the while there was one gentleman who was madly in love with my grandmother, but because this man was not a church-going individual, she rebuffed his attempts at romance and even an offer of marriage – more than once I might add.
>
> "When that same man finally got tired of waiting for my grandmother, he ended up marrying the preacher's sister! Needless to say, that crushed my grandmother but she had no one to blame but herself. Instead of following her own heart, she chose to listen to and put her faith in some preacher who was more interested in getting his weekly tithes than anything else. I made the decision at the age of 15 that I would not repeat the same mistakes

in my own life. There is a world of difference between having faith and being a blind follower." ~ Nichelle B.

Earlier, I described the three-step program in operation at black churches that is designed to keep the female congregation confused and wanting. Every woman who has failed to understand the difference between spirituality and religion has already allowed religion to control her thinking and fallen in line with Step One ("make the women believe they need to be led by a man").

Step Two ("brainwash the people you can get under your control") is demonstrated by T. D. Jakes in his 1993 best-seller *Woman, Thou Art Loosed!*, which launched his career and made him a household name in the black community. In the book he tells black women that they deserve better than what they have been getting, but that if they cannot find a suitable mate, Jesus will be their lover.

> "The Lord wants to make sweet love to you. I'm not being carnal, I'm being real. He wants to hold you. He wants you to come in at the end of the day and say, 'Oh, Lord, I could hardly make it today. . . . Hold me. Touch me. Strengthen me. Let me hold You. Let me bless You. I've set the night aside for us."

The dogma inherent in Step Three ("ostracize the people you can't") is the chief reason there so many single black women in church on their knees, praying for pie in the sky and a man that's never going to come through those doors. Admittedly, there are a small number of mega-churches that tout a male membership as high as 50 percent of the congregation; however we all know that being a member of a church on paper does not mean that you show up for services regularly, if at all.

Brothas may be God-fearing, but they are also leery of going to church because they know the game. The black male's suspiciousness of the male church leaders' honesty effectively ostracizes hundreds of thousands of strong-minded, together black men from church. Church and religion is actually designed to ensnare and control women. The brief essay below (penned in 1911 by Lemuel K. Washburn and published under the title *Is the Bible Worth Reading? And Other Essays*, explains the concept fully:

Christianity - a Woman's Religion

"The Christian church of today is the church of women. Woman is certainly the better-half of Christianity. She is the minister's right bower. The Christian soldier is an Amazon. The first at the prayer-meeting, at the donation party, at the missionary convention, at the Sunday service, at the altar, at the Sunday school is woman, and the last is woman, too. Without its female members, adherents and workers the Christian church would be an abandoned wreck within a week. It is true that men give money to the church, but they do it generally to please the women or at their solicitation.

"The Christian religion is a female religion. It is emotional piety. There is nothing robust, independent about it, nothing that appeals to strength, intellect, reason. It is a vine, not an oak. Even its chief idol was fashioned for female worship. The songs of Christianity were written for women to sing, rather than men. The God of Christianity is a father, its savior is a young man, and its angels are all of the masculine gender. The Christian heaven is a he-kingdom, as far as its administration is concerned -- a sort of celestial harem -- for certainly 10 women go there to one man, if the membership of the church determines the election of candidates to heavenly bliss. The two favorite hymns at the prayer-meeting, the two that are sung with most feeling, are 'Jesus, lover of my soul,' and 'Nearer, my God, to thee.'

"Religion was invented to catch women. The priest is the spider and woman the fly. Upon the altar of every faith woman has been the sacrifice. Religion claims its female victims in this age just as surely as when the Hindoo widow was sent to join her dead husband on wings of flame. Woman today is not killed to appease a God, but she is still made a fool of by the priest. The spirit of the offering is the same, the form, only, is different. The foundation of every Christian church is woman; the salary-raiser of every Christian minister is woman. Woman is the keystone in every arch of Christian endeavor that spans the earth. She is 'the bright, particular star' of the church's hope. Men are not so easily caught by the Christian scheme of salvation as women. They want to see some return for their money on earth. It is the woman who is caught in the religious toils; it is the woman who is the slave of God, the victim of priest and minister."

What Going to Church Won't Do for Single Black Women

Seeking to align yourself with a house of worship that elevates you spiritually while respecting your intellect should be a chief concern in selecting a church. A woman who believes anything she is told will be more likely to fall prey to the games of unscrupulous church leaders. Such a believer never questions anything she's told and lives her life based on what she calls "faith" but others call blind stupidity. No matter what a pastor says or what reasons you have been socialized to believe church is where you need to be, there are certain things you should not expect to find and certain perceived benefits you will not receive from church attendance.

(a) *Going to church will not get you the black man you seek and it never will.*

God is not a genie, and he will not gift you with a man. You have to actually place yourself in a position to meet single men. To find a man interested in marriage requires getting out of church and going to events and locations where single men of all races are. For many reasons that will be explained as we move forward, you will not find the man of your dreams in a black church because marriageable black men are not in church.

Many people believe that what I'm promoting is church as a "speed dating" event. They are adamant that women should not be going to church to look for a husband anyway: They are supposed to go to church to commune with God and hear The Word. Though I've never said that finding a man was the sole reason for a woman to go to church, I think such an expectation makes perfect sense.

If you are a single woman and your faith is important to you, you will go to your place of worship seeking guidance and counsel on selecting a mate. A woman who would be looking for a husband, someone with whom she is "equally yoked" – a man with whom she shares beliefs. Mature women want to have a husband, along with sex, children, love and a life. There is nothing wrong with wanting such things, especially as they are considered to be the preferred union in the eyes of God. So why would anyone criticize a single woman for seeking a man with a similar mindset in a church environment? After all, many single women are being told by their pastors to look for such a man in church, only in church, and only in HIS church.

> "I was speaking to a buddy of mine that just confirmed your article. He says he's a good man but DOESN'T MEET WOMEN IN CHURCH. Women should be able to look outside of the church and even date a guy that doesn't go to church at all, but they are too brainwashed because the church GUARANTEES that if they marry a man and both of them are devout Christians the marriage will be forever and happy. Then when the shit doesn't work out, the church throws them under the bus and says 'well they must not have really been walking in the word or else this wouldn't have happened!' " ~C. Williams

Though such thinking might make logical sense, my point is that you can look until you turn purple and break out in pink polka dots -- church is not where you are going to find your husband. The single men of quality that a woman would want to marry absolutely refuse to go to church.

> "I am a single Christian African-American woman in my mid-40s, and I rarely attend church anymore. Unfortunately I've found that a lot of so-called single Christian African-American men that I have dated are nothing but hypocrites.

"I decided nine years ago to become abstinent until I marry, and as a Christian I knew that I should not have been having premarital sex, but used to do it anyway. The main men I run across who have a problem with the fact that I don't have premarital sex are, you guessed it the 'Christian men!'

"I have lost count of how many of them had something negative to say to say, tried to change my mind, or just stopped calling me when I let them know I wasn't into premarital sex. And these were often men who claimed to be Christians and attend church pretty regularly or at least much more than I do. And I'm not talking about really young guys; I'm talking about men in their 40s and 50s.

"You would think that a Christian man would be able to appreciate and encourage a Christian woman to not be out here fornicating, and to try and live the way God wants us to according to the Bible. But instead, many of our African-American Christian men are turning their backs on that aspect of Christianity and on the Christian women who try to uphold those principals. Hey if I have that type of self-control that means that I have morals and self discipline and won't be out here cheating on you if we got married. Instead these Christian men turn to the loose women who will gratify them sexually without the ring or commitment, who are out here just doing what feels good with whomever they wanna do it with.

"Why claim you are a Christian when you are out here doing everything non-Christians and non-believers are doing? When a guy tells me he is a Christian I now know that usually doesn't include not fornicating; a lot of single Christian men conveniently forget about that verse in the Bible. This fact alone has made me loosen my dating requirements. I no longer feel that I should only date Christian men. God-fearing and/or spiritual is good enough for me." ~Joan K.

I believe her adjustment in expectations is realistic and smart. In any fishing expedition, odds for a successful catch are vastly improved when one casts a wider net.

(b) Going to church is not making you more attractive and interesting to single black men.

With the exception of those that go to church because it's a habit that carried over from childhood, people generally go to church looking for something because they are in need. If you are a happy, healthy, strong and confident person, you don't feel the need for church. Going to church is a lot like going to the hospital; healthy people don't go to the hospital, sick people go to hospitals to be healed. Church is where sick souls go to be healed. If your soul is not sick, if you are not looking for strength or in need of healing, you have no need for church.

Secondly, women deep in the church all think the same. There is little to no challenge to get a woman that is "in the church" as she spouts rhetoric and canned phrases *ad nauseam* all day long. Men enjoy a woman that is stimulating and mentally challenging, adventurous and creative -- traits women deeply indoctrinated into church culture generally don't offer.

"I told my daughter a man in the church is no better than the man in the street, and sometimes the man in the street may be better cuz at least he is not frontin! I am not saying all men in church are bad, but too many are gay, have wives and are having affairs with women in the congregation; some have even gotten women pregnant from affairs. It's totally scandalous and everyone knows what's going on but they still come to the church and listen to that man every Sunday. Something is wrong with black women when it comes to church. I think your article is 100 percent on point. I have a sister who gives money to the church, but won't pay her phone or electric bill. Her house is a wreck and sometimes she doesn't have money for food, but is shouting she loves the Lord every Sunday in 'chuuch.' " ~Marquet J.

Many single black men also report having serious conflicts when dating a woman that is into "chuuch" because she tries to convert him or flatly dismisses him if he refuses to attend church. Men find such women to be run-of-the-mill, predictable and not at all inspiring.

If the only book you read is the Bible, you will not be interesting to men. If the only outings or events you attend are church-related, you will not be interesting to men. If you think oral sex or walking around naked in front of your man is freaky, weird or sinful, you will not be interesting to men. If everything and everyone is viewed through the lenses of your "faith" with no tolerance for people who are different, you will not be interesting to men. If the clothes and shoes you wear look like they belong to your grandmother, you will not be interesting to men. If you are quick to regurgitate what "Pastor said" instead of what you think and what you know will work for your relationship, men are likely to find you to be more work than pleasure, so they leave you alone.

(c) *Going to church is not where you are going to find eligible bachelors to date.*

Though there may be many young males in your church attending with their mothers and a few mature men that occasionally wander through the doors, it is unlikely that you will find a large number of single black men of age in black churches. When I say "large number" I mean a number of men on a par with the number of single women in a church interested in and available for marriage.

Interestingly enough, this is not as much of an issue in churches that have a large population of non-black members. Jewish, Asian and Latin men are socialized to expect to marry, as becoming a family man is an integral part of their culture. Among other races, marriage is a foundational component of manhood, and young boys are expected to grow up, acquire a wife, have a family and take care of that family. However, in the black community males are not receiving similar messages. While growing up black males receive the message that marriage is a shackle, a noose around their neck, and something to be avoided at all costs.

Black men and women are polar opposites when it comes to socialization about commitment and marriage. Black males are told by other men that all sistahs are gold diggers out to take their money and property. Black men are also told that women are to be used for sex and discarded, that the child support system is against them, and that it is better to be single and free of all emotional entanglements. At the same time black females are being socialized to revere marriage, to elevate any brotha to the status of demigod, and to believe that they are failures unless they "have a man."

Sadly, men rarely examine their belief systems when it comes to relationships, instead operating on auto-pilot by playing games, avoiding emotional closeness, fleeing from commitment and refusing to truly love. Black men prefer to place the blame on feminism (again blaming women) for their lack of respect for women and marriage. Thus, women experience nothing but temporary, shallow relationships with black men that play at love for awhile, then dance away to the next, then the next, leaving a string of fatherless children and broken hearts in their wake.

Why Independent Black Women Settle for Less

Women are stimulated by men that exude confidence, and most confident men have a substantial amount of influence and power. From the ghetto fabulous hoochie dating the neighborhood's biggest drug dealer, to the White House intern performing oral sex with the President, power is an aphrodisiac to women. The most powerful man in most black neighborhoods is the pastor of the largest church, the man that wields considerable political influence in the community, as well as moral and financial influence over the lives of thousands of individuals in it. Even the most violent gang bangers give at least a grudging level of respect to God and men of God; therefore they rarely do their dirt in or around churches.

With women filling the pews of most black churches, the tithes and offerings this spiritual leader receives during every Bible study and church service are directly from the purses and paychecks of females. The mentality that directs women to be overly-giving "helpmeets" plays out in one-sided romantic relationships women have with black men as well. Most black women believe only a selfish gold digger would demand that a man prove himself to be self sufficient and able to provide for her and any children the two may have. The unwillingness of black women to be viewed as needing anything from a man has created several generations of Sistahs that over function in all of their relationships with the opposite sex.

Some of this can be attributed to the fact that black men have lagged behind in education and economic growth, requiring that black women step in and assume the reigns. After all, children need food, clothing and shelter; if their father cannot due to illness or imprisonment meet his obligations and responsibilities to his children, someone has to do it! However, I believe the primary reason black women "do too much" is because they are afraid of what will happen if they don't.

Black women take great pride in being independent and wear the title of Independent Black Woman like a badge of honor. The ability to pay their own way, handle their business by themselves and take care of others without asking a man for a dime is extremely important to them. However, these same women are often depleted mentally, physically and financially. It's exhausting to be the breadwinner, cook, chauffeur, maid and washerwoman for an entire family. They really can't be angry though, because they allowed healthy, well-employed men to be uninvolved and lazy by picking up the reigns he laid down instead of leaving them lying there.

On the flip side are the black women who refuse to play the "I'm an Independent Black Woman Game". These women see that there is no prize to be won by overburdening one's self with responsibility, so they opt to be less independent in the traditional gender role of a submissive female. Their hope is that this traditional mindset and willingness to follow a man's lead will position them as a better pick when it comes to selection of a wife. But that doesn't really work either. This dichotomy has created two distinct types of single black women:

>(a) **The Independent Black Woman** is suspicious of any man that comes in wanting to do for her. Usually this is because she has either been trained not to depend on men because they rarely come through, or she has been in a position to be dependent upon a man that disappointed her when he didn't meet his obligations. So as an adult, she struggles with even allowing a nice stranger to buy her a drink at a party or club for fear that he will "want something" that she is not prepared to give. She does not want to feel obligated to any man ever, about anything. When a man, trying to show her a good time takes her out, she insists on paying "her share" or "helping" him with the expenses of the date that he asked her out on. Ever protective of their feelings and fearful of dependency on a type that has in the past always proven undependable, the Independent Black Woman will let it be known "I don't NEED YOU!" Some men feel insulted and/or emasculated by this type of behavior and withdraw emotionally from the woman

they love. Their attitude is, "Since she wants to do everything, I'm going to let her!" Not seeing the set up and the vicious cycle that they've established for themselves, these women go into relationships never expecting to be given to or cherished. Their men become lazy and complacent because no demands for giving are ever placed upon them. Even if she should ask him for something, he is so resentful of being pushed away in the past that he will most often refuse to comply. Should he opt to at least pretend to do what she asks, he'll perform in a rudimentary, unenthusiastic way that frustrates or angers her. She steps in to do it "the right way" herself, which was what he wanted to manipulate her into doing in the first place.

(b) **The Helpless Black Woman** is emotionally and psychologically needy, and possibly financially needy as well. She seeks a relationship or a man as the one missing ingredient in her world that will make her life complete. In her mind, a man will make everything right and save her from a life of loneliness and despair. Many religious women fall into this category, as they seek to have the husband that "God meant for me" and subscribe to the Christian principle of female submission to a male. Once she is partnered, even if it's with a fool, she feels positively defined. Believing she is nothing on her own, she sees herself as someone only when she is Mrs. X, or So and So's woman. She stays in relationships where she is being mistreated, lied to, cheated on or abused, because in her mind any relationship is better than no relationship at all. She also believes that love means pain and struggle, and that she must be devoted to her man at all costs. These are the same women that will look down her nose at The Independent Black Woman with a critical sneer. She'll say snarky things like "that's why you're single!" or "that's why you can't get or keep a man!" in an attempt to establish herself and her position in life as superior to that of any single female.

Many Christian females start off as the Helpless Black Woman, then morph into the Independent Black Woman. This change usually occurs after she has been hurt by, abused or abandoned by a series of men that turned out not to be her savior Boaz, but instead just another Dumbaz.

(d) Going to church is not going to teach you to be fiscally responsible, investment savvy, or empower you to achieve greatness as a single woman.

Statistics (posted on the http://www.america.gov/ website) state that $96.82 billion dollars was donated to churches nationwide in the year 2006. (That is the latest year for which figures are available on this site.) Tyler Media Services estimates that black churches pulled in $17 billion of that $96.82 total. During that same year, the Atlanta Journal Constitution reported that Creflo Dollar's World Changers reported $69 million in 2006 income all by itself.

LiveSteenz Research complied statistics that narrow the focus to revenues generated by the nation's black churches. Their report indicates that more than $420 billion flowed through black churches in the 20 year period of 1980-2000.

All non-profit organizations are required to file an IRS form 990, which shows how much money was received and what its expenditures were. Any non-profit organization must make this form available on request. Yet, under the IRS Code, churches are excluded from filing a 990 tax form, or any other form that exposes their income and expenses. The IRS is prohibited by law from inspecting the books of churches to determine where the contributions go or how the churches spend the money they collect.

What this means is that churches may claim to be charitable organizations, but no one knows for sure how much of the billions they receive each year actually goes to charity or to build more church buildings and replace roofs, or to be used as the preacher's personal piggy bank. Despite the fact that there are 2-3 churches every mile in the inner city, there is little evidence of even a few thousand dollars being poured into surrounding black communities by these churches. All you do know with any certainty is that you give, and your pastor is happy to receive.

Thousands of black churches nationwide are filled with smart, well-educated, financially savvy women who can band together and form groups that invest in the stock market, utilities, mutual funds or real property. With 20 women investing 7 percent of their annual income (let's use a figure of $40,000) to the fund, that is $56,000 per year. Over a 10-year period that is $560,000 invested. Add to that figure interest on cash deposits, dividends, stock splits and appreciation - our group may easily have $1 million of capital to work with in short order. Should you tithe to your financial group the 10 percent you were giving to a church, that figure would increase accordingly.

Why would you give your money to a church where you have no knowledge of how it is used, when you could instead use your money to directly benefit your children, or to benefit charities and scholarship funds that have personal significance for you?

If sistah's can support churches to the tune of $420 billion in 20 years, it means that black women can get together on their own and do magnificent things for themselves, their immediate communities and their children. You do not need a man to manage your money for you through church donations where you see no return on your investment and have no idea where the money is actually going.

(e) Going to church is not going to broaden your horizons, make you more tolerant and accepting of those that are different.

Church members are frequently characterized as being very judgmental and gossipy. When trying to explain the negative behavior of one member of their clan, Christians have been quick to throw each other under the bus by saying, "Well you know that person is not a TRUE Christian," as if their assessment of the individual's behavior is the final authority, not God's.

There also seems to be an air of exclusivity among many Christians, as if they believe "my church or walk or being makes me a better Christian and closer to God than yours does!" On one hand we're told that you can pray for forgiveness, be saved, that Christians bring others to the light, blah blah blah, but little to no such tolerance is shown for someone that has lost their way. Insignificant efforts are made to bring lost lambs back into the flock. Instead, the lost are condemned, derided and, in some churches, shunned for making a mistake.

If a spirit of forgiveness and desire to help those that are not yet in the church but need its steadying influence is not being promoted in black churches, then what is the focus and the reason for your church's existence? You should think about that and come up with some solid answers for yourself.

(f) Going to church is not going to encourage you to be free of the chains of patriarchy and oppression of your feminine energy.

When my article *The Black Church: How The Black Church Keeps African American Women Single and Lonely* first hit the blogosphere, I encountered a great deal of angry commentary from the deeply religious Christian community. One visitor to the blog that identified himself as Reverend Graves posted the following comment:

> "Christianity isn't about dating. It is about Jesus - Jesus who made women a central part of His work on Earth. Admittedly the Christian church has become an institution that in many places drifts from the priorities set by our Savior, but the church is about saving souls from the condemnation of sin and changing lives for the better. Church is not meant to be the place for people to hook up, so judging the worth of a house of worship on a sister's chance of meeting Mr. Right is missing the whole point. It would be like a gunshot victim selecting an emergency room based on the likelihood of finding a boyfriend or an unemployed person applying for jobs

only at places where there is a high percentage of potential mates.

"Consider the connection between the absence of black men in church and the absence of "good" black men in general. Church is not the cause of the problem but rather an indicator of the true cause. The lack of a spiritual foundation and spiritual maturity that leads brothers to devalue women, to abandon a sense of honor, and to live self-destructive lives is the same malaise that leads them to discount the faith. In theology we call this 'sin.'

"If the objective is to liberate women from the legacy of patriarchal oppression, telling them to make 'finding a man' the center of their universe seems counterproductive. If even a sister's spiritual path is dictated by the hunt for a man, then you make all men god to all women. (Now who's preaching submission?)"
~Reverend Graves

In response to the reverend, I explained that Christianity and all religions are very much about dating and partnership. Every religion focuses on establishing a strong foundation for a spiritual marriage between a man and a woman for the purpose of creating a family via sex and children within marriage. Single women in church have every right to ask why there are not more normal, healthy, finally savvy, socially responsible black men in the churches, and why the pews are filled with lonely single women.

Certainly there are problems with the black men in the community. But since the church has always been the cornerstone of the black community that established guidelines and provided spiritual guidance, if these young men are lawless and rude, whose responsibility is it if not that of the church? Too many black church leaders are like Reverend Graves -- throwing up their hands instead of rolling up their sleeves.

Single Black Men Are Not in Church and It's Not an Accident

I've often been asked what black churches are or should be doing to help young black males. The answer to what they ARE doing on a large scale is a big fat nothing at all! Sure, there are black churches here and there in cities across the nation that have a program that operates in their one neighborhood, but I'm talking about an organized, focused effort launched by black churches across the nation to save black men before they need the prison ministry or the coroner.

Black men are killing themselves off. According to news reports, at least 52 people were shot between Friday evening and early Monday in Chicago the weekend of June 21, 2010. The number of people shot over the 2011 Labor Day weekend in New York City totaled 43. Violence among young men is at an all time high around the nation. The one group of already established organizations poised to step in and do something about it? Black Christian church organizations. However, black churches will never step up to do anything to help young black males *en masse*, because there is no benefit to the men running churches to do so.

The black church has abdicated its responsibility to young black men and women and left them to hang out to dry on their own. There is a church on just about every corner in most black communities but with all the money churches take in every week, what are they doing to change things? Church leaders may believe that they are not the cause of the problem; I say they are the direct cause.

The answer lies in what is required of a man when he goes to church. No man wants to be forced to check his masculinity at the door when he walks into a church. However, once a man sets foot inside a church house he is expected to drop to his knees, admit that he is nothing, and say that he loves some other guy. He would also have to let the man standing in front of the church in a position of power over everyone in that building tell him what to do, which means allowing that man to have an amazing amount of influence over his life. Men on the whole are not going to let that happen. They are just not going to roll that way. Submission on your knees and admitting love for another man is contradictory to the concept of manhood that black men have been socialized to believe makes them men. Plus, it's kinda gay.

Black men are taught to stand strong and to stand alone, to figure out their own problems and take care of their own business. Black men hate to see doctors, to take medication, and absolutely refuse to invest in psychotherapy. So, if you have a guy pressured to go to church and admit that he doesn't have his stuff together, he will resist. He believes that giving up his autonomy will make him weak; he will then be on a par with several hundred women and that will make him feel even weaker.

How can he be considered a man if he is feels that he is on a par with women, the very people he is supposed to be stronger than, that he is supposed to lead and protect? This is especially true if he is in any way suspicious of the pastor and his motives. Brothas are not usually trying to mess up somebody else's pimp game, but that doesn't mean they are going to play the game, so they just stay away.

Every black church in the nation has more single female members than single males. In some it's reported to be as high as 60:1. The men that ARE in church are either older, married, gay or useless because they are in a12-step program of some sort, or fresh out of prison. Don't fool yourself into thinking that this demographic is an accident. Churches are structured to have one man in power, one rooster in charge of the hen house! What purpose would the black church serve if black men got their shit together *en masse*? If that were to happen, I believe that the roof would be yanked off the hen-house and organized religion would be exposed as the fraud it is.

Reality is that there is no benefit to "passa" to have virile, financially solvent, young and handsome men that would be attractive to the single women in his church. Men want to come into any situation and have decision-making power and influence. That is not a privilege that will be afforded to young males in black churches. Testosterone filled young males challenge older males, they don't generally listen to or follow other men unless they are fearful for some reason (as a violent gang leader). Should a strong young male draw a woman's attention to himself vs. passa, it means passa loses power and influence. The more males in his church attracting women's attention, the more power and influence he loses, and passa doesn't want that.

This is the sole reason why few church dollars are spent on programs that will help young black men become better people, become leaders, to increase their confidence and self esteem, or help them to get their stuff together. Churches with millions of dollars in their coffers have not established private high schools or small colleges. Neither have they established job training programs to teach young men how to work on cars or diesel engines, do cabinetry electronics plumbing or carpentry, or to build or repair computers – all job skills that will allow them to feel good about themselves, become productive citizens and get them off the streets. There are few church-sponsored programs established to teach young black males anything except how to read a Bible.

Instead, the focus of churches is on dominating and controlling women -- teaching women how to be fundraisers and cooks for the church, and wives, mothers, and "helpmeets" to the non-existent mates pastors preach women should stay in church to wait on.

The game set out above shows in detail how I know none of these pastors are really serious about getting the single women married to loving husbands. Their power lies in having a church full of women, filling their heads full of dreams and taking their money. That is all they really want to do. Black church society is built around black male ministers. No title holder really wants a strong contender to challenge their position, though they may give lip service to the contrary.

If a woman thinks a husband would make her feel complete as she has been raised to believe, and she wants a man that holds a similar belief system, then she should have that man. Each religious leader, each church pastor or minster needs to be doing all he can to make sure that all avenues to achieve that blessing are open to the women of his congregation, not blocked for the convenience and financial gain of the church.

The Five Types of Single Men That Do Go to Church

The principles of manhood require that a man stand on his own two feet, and that he meet life's challenges without asking for help from anyone else. This means that no man of strength and purpose is going to go to church and have some other man judge him, tell him that he is wrong or bad, or tell him what to do. Therefore, you can bet if a young, handsome, strapping man is in church every single Sunday just like you are, the likelihood that there is something wrong with him is pretty high.

Some women will argue that there are lots of "nice" single men in church and that I am being harsh. Okay, I've visited dozens of churches around the country and looked hard at those guys in attendance. Without a doubt I can tell you flatly that the vast majority (I'm saying 98 percent) of them fit into one of five categories:

1. **A loser working a 12-step program.** These guys are in church looking for structure and something to believe in besides themselves, because they are weak and confused. Church is probably where they SHOULD be; they need help getting their lives back on track and are seeking solace and comfort in God. If they can hook up with a woman looking desperately for a church-going man of any ilk, they've got it made. But if you are not in a 12-step program

yourself, do you really need to be with a man whose sense of manhood is so shaky? Can you trust that he won't take you down with him when he falls off the wagon and it rolls over him? You deserve a man that is solid and stable – someone you can depend on and grow with, not someone looking for strength just to make it through the day.

2. **Openly or in the closet gay men, neither of which is interested in marrying.** Some closeted gay men are wrestling with severe guilt and confusion about their desires, which they hope to pray away in church. Some we might identify as bisexual, in that they may be married or involved in relationships with women, while dabbling with men on "the down low." Others are openly gay and attend church seeking acceptance from a conservative community that generally turns its nose up at homosexuality (in spite of popular jokes about gay choir directors in black churches). A gay man in church may also be seeking forgiveness for his sins, though he has no intention of avoiding having the same fun next Friday night if not sooner. Many of the guys in this category have been locked up in prison for years. Though they were not gay when they went into the joint, you can bet some dabbling in homosexuality went on, whether it was consensual or not. Whatever may be this guy's issue, he is emotionally and psychologically unavailable for the type of relationship a heterosexual woman seeking a husband holds as her ideal.

3. **Child molesting pedophiles seeking victims or fighting their urges.** In every city there are thousands of adult men that, for whatever reason, are

unable to form healthy, age-appropriate sexual relationships with other adults. These men, called pedophiles, are sexually stimulated by pornographic images and/or fantasies of sex with children; however, once a pedophile crosses over to sexual contact with an actual child, they become a child molester. Though cases involved priests in the Catholic Church are widely publicized in news media, the Christian Science Monitor reports that "most American churches being hit with child sexual-abuse allegations are Protestant, and most of the alleged abusers are not clergy or staff, but church volunteers." Though grossly underreported, statistics show an average of 70 cases of child molestation reported to police that occurred in churches every month. For a woman with small children of her own or in her extended family, a man with this type of sexual drive is an extremely poor and very dangerous choice for a mate.

4. **Opportunistic players on the prowl.** Every player I know attends several different churches, some of them go regularly. Well-dressed, well-employed, tall dark and handsome, they are excellent at the games they run on women. Though most spread their talents around, there are a couple of them that have more than one woman in the same congregation! Since sex amongst unmarried singles is a sin, it is easy for him to gain the assurance of each woman that she will keep their little tête-à-tête's secret lest they feel the wrath of the pastor. This secrecy makes it easy for him to hide the fact that he is bed hopping with four or five single ladies, right under their respective

noses. Opportunistic players have easy pickings among the hundreds of horny, lonely single women that will cook, provide them with free meals, money and gifts, and satisfy his sexual urges in the hopes getting of a marriage proposal (though these players have no intention of marrying and committing to anyone).

5. **Elderly widowers, cat daddies and reformed players**. The players and cat daddies have played themselves so hard and so long, they're worn out. For them, playtime is over so they start their search for a wife in church. The widowers show up in church because their wife of 35 years recently passed away, and they are looking for companionship and someone to take care of them for the remaining years of their life. Worried about dying alone, both types bring their behinds back to church to find a "good Christian woman" for marriage. Essentially they are looking for a free nursemaid and bed warmer without too much mileage -- someone relatively untouched by other men. They want a woman that can cook and clean, someone to provide comfort and take care of their old, broken-down asses before they die. It's not about finding a woman that believes in Jesus as much as it is finding a woman with a particular mentality: They're both seeking a woman that will do what he wants her to do because she firmly believes in male superiority and female submission. What better place to find such a woman than a black church?

In spite of the facts laid out above, single black women go to church week after week, hearing over and over again the message that they should be seeking "a God-fearing man." Though your pastor may tell you that there should be no room in your life for a man without faith in The Lord, my advice is that you not put all your faith in someone just because he goes to church. A woman must never glorify a man based solely on his gender or because he sits next to you in church holding a Bible and saying "bless you, sistah!" Common sense must prevail in every aspect of life.

With so few single black men attending church, and those that are in church being largely unsuitable as marital partners, what is it that single black women are really looking for in church? Why do black women run to church in droves and willingly put themselves in the position to be dictated to, harshly judged and instructed like a child on how to live their lives by some man that is not their father and to whom they are not married?

Marriage - The Carrot at the End of the Stick

"Harriet Tubman said if she could have freed 1000 more slaves, if she could have just convinced them that they were slaves. That's the way I see (black) womanhood. We still seem to be confused as to what our status has become. And we are steadily seeking happiness, in a set up that was never meant to make us happy." ~ Brooklyn Blue Bird

Black women have totally bought into notions of male supremacy and patriarchal thinking; few seem to truly grasp the impact those belief systems have on their lives once married. Each step the bride-to-be takes as she walks down the aisle is another step toward loss of individuality and self-mastery. Though some brides and grooms have eliminated the traditional vow that declares "I now pronounce you MAN AND WIFE", the mentality about a woman's proper role as a "wife" has remained unchanged for centuries. Once the ceremony is over and she turns to face her guests, her identity as a woman of the

21st century is gone; she is now linked inextricably to her husband as his sub-set with the title "Mr. and Mrs. Benjamin Clark".

In black church society there seems to be a default set of expectations that mandates that "wife" equals "loss of separate identity." Those men and women who defend these trite traditions fail to understand that society's view of marriage means the woman that you call your wife has just given up her freedom, her autonomy, and a part of her soul so that her husband can have exclusive sexual rights to her body and reproductive system. In exchange she is supposed to get comfort and security, but with women being required to work outside the home in most black families just to make ends meet, she is actually supplying her own security. Men take their wives for granted too, so there is little real comfort offered. It's more a figment of women's imagination.

Black men as a group are great adherents to the notion that taking a wife means you have a person that you now have full ownership of. Husbands, frustrated with their wife's resistance to an idea believe "she must do it because she is MY WIFE!" Black men also hate the idea that a woman would insist on keeping her given surname after marriage, railing on and on about the negative impact of feminism on marriages "when women used to take pride in being homemakers," condemning feminism as the primary cause of problems in black male/female relationships.

Marriage requires a great deal of sacrifice for women, and is generally exhausting, thankless work. I've often wondered why black women continue to think marriage is something they really need.

Being the nurturers of mankind, black women relish the role of "helper." She is not regarded as a leader or pushed to achieve anything other than to be a servant, mother, lover or wife. She may hold a PhD, but because she is helping her church, her pastor or her husband achieve a goal and purpose, she puts herself second, third and last.

The negative impact of marriage on black women was documented in a 2005 study by the Institute for American Values. The study entitled *Consequences of Marriage for African Americans* concluded: "Overall, Black women appear to benefit from marriage substantially less than do White women. By contrast, the differences in the benefit from marriage between Black men and White men appear in most cases to be minimal." Another interesting finding concerned the health of married African-American women, stating: "While both Black men and Black women receive a marriage premium, this premium in most cases appears to be larger for men. Put a bit differently, Black women overall seem to receive less benefit from marriage than do Black men. This gender gap is especially pronounced in the areas of family life and physical health. In fact, married Black women actually report *poorer* health than do unmarried Black women."

Married women are often the most haggard looking, the least put together, and the most overweight and physically out of shape women you will see. It's difficult if not impossible for a woman not to lose herself in marriage, slipping, almost unconsciously into behaviors (roles) that both she and her husband have never examined or questioned. Therefore, he expects and thinks it natural for a woman to give up her dreams in order to be married to him, as HE becomes her top priority.

A married woman also gives up her time, sacrifices her figure, and puts her life as an individual on hold to meet her husband's expectations. Becoming the submissive wife of a black man means a woman must:

- keep house the way he likes it
- cook the type of food he likes
- cook the food in the manner he prefers
- avoid talking to his male friends so you aren't labeled "too flirty"
- have meals ready to suit his schedule
- ask his permission before you do things
- never question his decisions or "talk back"
- have sex when and how he likes it
- name the children you carried for nine months the way he wants
- spend or save money the way he tells you to
- live where he thinks you should
- do all the tasks that he decides are beneath him or 'your job'
- hang out with your friends only during the time he allots for your recreation
- associate only with friends/family that meet his approval
- never say you are too tired to have sex or do anything else he wants you to do
- dress in the manner he deems appropriate in public and private
- never voice a controverting opinion that makes him wrong and you right

Churches that emphasize traditional gender roles in marriage greatly contribute to female unhappiness and divorce. National divorce statistics report that between 70-90 percent of the nation's divorces are initiated by women miserable in their marriages (Am. Law & Economics Review, 2000). Obviously, there is something about traditional marriage that does not meet women's true needs after the wedding fantasy fades and reality sets in.

Equalitarian marriages where couples have a balance of power and equal responsibility produce happier wives, happier children and fewer divorces long-term. However, equality in decision making and a balance of power is not a part of the marriage discussion in black churches; instead, emphasis is repeatedly placed on female submission and being the "neck" to her husband's "head."

Married women should examine the structure of their unions, and ask themselves if rigid gender roles have contributed to their exhaustion and unhappiness. Black women must begin to challenge the religious-based institutions that contribute to their dissatisfaction and misery. Question the TRUE purpose of marriage as is expected of you per church doctrine, and ask yourself: "Is this really what I need in my life?" If the answer is negative, have the courage to discuss making the changes you need to be happy in marriage with your current or future husband.

Too Educated, Too Materialistic and Too Undesirable

Church leaders and the women that attend black churches can make a woman with a great career, and educational or political aspirations feel less than successful if she is unmarried. No one at church ever asks about the big case she won, congratulates her on her recent promotion, or asks how she is doing in the polls. Instead their focus is "why hasn't somebody snatched you up yet?" or "don't you want to get married and have children?" Even her own family, church goers themselves, will treat her accomplishments as insignificant compared to acquisition of a husband.

A woman with higher aspirations than to change diapers and do laundry for other people is looked down upon in many churches. Such a woman may even be considered a bad influence on those that are singularly focused on being a submissive wife and pleasing a man.

After all, women hear black men say over and over that successful, unmarried black women are too educated, too aggressive, too materialistic, or not submissive enough. Single women that place high value on higher education are often the brunt of snide remarks and sneering put downs by less educated black men that warn "none of that is going to make you a better WIFE."

The underlying threat is that you must stay quiet and in your envelope if you want to have any hope of marrying a black man. You will be threatened with being alone unless you stop trying to compete with men by acquiring more formal education, or by making more money than your man does. You must listen to men, and you need to do all of this without asking men any questions or making any demands on them to give back to you.

This is a classic set-up where single black women are "damned if you do and damned if you don't." Confused about what to do when faced with so many challenging choices, many women opt not to rock the boat so they don't do anything. Many women are so fearful of making the wrong choice and alienating themselves from the mate selection process that they choose the known evil. So they continue doing the same thing they've been doing for years – waiting and praying and biting their tongue.

But none of that really matters for the single black woman in church seeking love; odds are poor that she will find a man in a black church setting anyway. Further complicating matters, many single women are in church for women's group, Bible study twice per week, some special committee meetings, singles ministry, fellowshipping through the community, and attending service all day on Sunday. When exactly is it that this single woman would have time for a man in her life? In reality she doesn't, which is just what the men in leadership at her church want!

> "As a single black female, by choice, I refuse to go to traditional black churches, especially those led by men. My wake up call came when a fight broke out in the church in which women turned over pews in anger when the pastor introduced his fiancée and soon to be wife. All of these single black women were in fact waiting on this pastor to marry them, because he was secretly dating ALL of them. This is just one of many situations that keep me out of their presence. I find the information slanted and geared towards men's favor, more than mine as a woman.

"There was even a minister in my home town that was on the news, pairing young single black women with ex-convicts. These men were beating these young girls, impregnating them with 6-7 children, literally keeping these women barefoot and pregnant. While the females worked and paid all the bills, these guys had multiple other women. If this is what being holy is all about, I'd rather be sinful!" ~ Christina B.

Black women should abandon traditional black churches that support male superiority, instead focusing on themselves, their needs and the needs of their children vs. those of black men. Any church or religious dogma used by men to castigate and control women should be thrown out. Beware of the wolf in sheep's clothing! Reality is that most black churches are nothing but a cover for the biggest scam and the longest running con game ever played.

6

CHURCHIANITY!
THE ONLY LEGITIMATE CON
GAME IN TOWN

Women are taken to the bank in the name of God, happily dancing to the Pied Piper's merry tune toward their own destruction

All religion, my friend, is simply evolved out of fraud, fear, greed, imagination, and poetry
~ Edgar Allan Poe (1809-1849)

The Business of Churching

I have been asked many times how I came to the conclusion that churching is a business, and that the business of church is nothing but a con game. "Where are your statistics to back that statement up?" they frequently demand to know.

One hundred percent of the time, the persons seeking statistics, charts, graphs and validation of a woman's statements from an outside source are black men. Their goal is of course to discredit what you say as a mere woman, unless what you say can be verified by another, preferable white, male. If they can successfully discredit you as a person, they will feel justified in dismissing what you have to say, no matter how valid it is. This type of behavior is known as an *ad hominem* attack. In case you are unfamiliar with the term, it goes like this:

(1) Woman makes claim XYZ.

(2) Man makes an attack on Woman's character, gender, marital status, presumed sexuality, weight, income, education, etc. without addressing claim XYZ at all.

(3) Therefore Woman's claim of XYZ is false

At this point in my life, these types of games and deflections amuse me. No matter what spin is put on my words, the facts cannot be denied -- church and the whole game of religion is a con game. I have empirical evidence that proves it.

How is Church a Con Game?

The term "con game" is a slang reference for what is called a "confidence game.'" Confidence games have been around for centuries. The gypsies are notorious for running them on people using the roofing and siding industry. Africans also use them -- you know those emails you get saying they need to use your bank account to collect an inheritance through a solicitor in London? One of the most popular cons used against seniors is called the Pigeon Drop, where someone claims to have found a bag of cash and is willing to split it with you, but only if you put up earnest money of as much as $15,000 first. That is another example of a con game.

However, religion is the #1 con game of all because it is the only game sanctioned by the government so it's perfectly legal. Church members and their churches have been targeted for fleecing for hundreds of millions of dollars by con artists blindly accepted to be Christ-like. A recent and far-reaching con was executed on members of Bishop Eddie Long's New Birth Baptist Church:

> *Former businessman Ephren Taylor was accused in federal court of luring worshipers at primarily black churches, including Eddie Long's New Birth Ministries, into investing in a scheme where he diverted their money into his own pockets. Taylor allegedly swindled more than $11 million while he was chief executive of North Carolina-based City Capital Corporation, according to the complaint filed in Atlanta in April 2012 by the SEC.*
>
> *He told investors their money would be used to support small businesses such as juice bars and gas stations, but instead regulators*

said the funding went to publicize Taylor's books, hire consultants and even finance his wife's singing career.

Bishop Eddie Long and his New Birth Missionary Baptist megachurch, were accused in a Georgia civil lawsuit of encouraging church members to invest in a scheme that promised 20 percent annual returns on safe investments but diverted their money to a failing company. Long's church marketed, sponsored and hosted "Wealth Tour Live" seminars in October 2009 which has been referred to as a Ponzi scheme orchestrated by Taylor. Long and his church both received compensation from Mr. Taylor, according to the complaint.

The government's complaint against Taylor also accuses him of duping clergy into giving him the pulpit on Sundays and bilking parishioners out of their hard-earned money with fraudulent promises. The lawsuits charge that the 29-year-old Taylor is a con artist who targeted worshipers in at least five East Coast states since 2004.

Using Your Fears Against You

When I was a child my father taught me that there are two kinds of people in the world – those motivated by the pursuit of pleasure, acquisition and power, and those motivated by avoidance of pain, hurt and devastation. A small percentage of the population (he estimated no more than 20 percent) fit into the former classification, with the vast majority of people (80 percent) in the latter category. Since most people want to avoid getting hurt at all costs, it's pretty easy to figure out how to scare them into doing what you want them to do.

"In the church where we have much freedom and independence we must get rid of preachers who are not prepared to help the people whom they exploit. The public must refuse to support men of this type. Ministers who are the creations of the old educational system must be awakened, and if this is impossible they must be dethroned. Those who keep the people in ignorance and play upon their emotions must be exiled. The people have never been taught what religion is, for most of the preachers find it easier to stimulate the superstition which develops in the unenlightened mind. Religion in such hands, then, becomes something with which you take advantage of weak people. Why try to enlighten the people in such matters when superstition serves just as well for exploitation?" ~Carter G. Woodson

Most often the con artist will use fear as his weapon of choice. The first step in the con game is the setup – the con artist has to determine if you are a mark. It's extremely easy to mark religious people because they talk about Jesus and God all the time. If someone believes in God and Jesus, it's a no-brainer to figure out that they also believe in hell and Satan. Church women are easily manipulated by referencing any of those four words hinting of a spiritual punishment for lack of compliance. If someone references a few Scriptures and throws in a few Biblical quotes and amen's, most church folk lose their minds and believe whatever comes out of that individual's mouth. If a man throws in a few "Praise the Lords!" the con artist is in there. Once they have gained your trust (your *con*fidence), they exploit it to their benefit.

Once the con artist knows what you want most, it is easy to coerce you into performing certain acts and behaving in specific ways using your fears against you. In church, the pastors use your fear of eternal damnation, of being single and alone forever, or loss of God's favor and blessings if you don't do as your pastor says you should. Most women – men, too – will comply out of anxiety and fear to the stated requests. After all, who wants to burn in hell forever and lose favor with God?

Once, the con artist knows your weakness and has coerced your cooperation through use of fear, when he asks you to give him money for whatever reason he creates (to allay your fears), you happily give it to him. Giving to churches expecting to get your share of the found money on the back side is nothing but a long-term pigeon drop scam.

> *Pastor Howard Richmond, 49, was charged in May 2010 with three felony counts of theft by deception for allegedly bilking three men, including one member of his Life Ministries church in Aurora Illinois, out of more than $470,000. The arrest came after a year-long investigation begun when a 60-year-old Skokie doctor who is a member of the congregation at Life Ministries, accused the pastor of swindling him out of $400,000 between December 2008 and March 2009. The doctor said that Richmond approached him following a service about investing money to help purchase the shopping center property where the storefront church is located, and to help fund the building of a new church. Richmond allegedly used the same ruse to deceive a 43-year-old Aurora man with whom he had a previous business relationship out of $8,000 in May 2009; and a 64-year-old Chicago dentist who had purchased some church-related DVDs, out of more than $67,000 between July and August of 2009. No one knows what he did with the money.*

Breaking Down the Pimp Game of Churching

What credentials does one need to have in order to become a Head Pastor of a church? None! Though some ministers go the educational route and acquire a B.A./B.S., M.A. or Doctor of Divinity degree from an accredited college or university, that isn't the path most religious leaders in the black community take. All you have to do to head up a black church is be a fast talker, have some game, and possess charisma so that women with money are attracted to you. If a pastor is single and handsome, that's a major plus.

Recently, a young man expressed to me his belief that churches start when people begin gathering together in their homes to pray and read Scripture.

No, that's not at all how churches start.

The idea of starting a church is usually spawned shortly after an arrest. While locked up behind bars, our future pastor realizes that spending years in prison is not his cup of tea. There has to be an easier, legal way to con people out of their money while giving them something in exchange that is viewed as legitimate.

He racks his brain to come up with an idea. One day he does a checklist of his skills and realizes that he has a commanding presence, plenty of game, an understanding of what motivates people to do what he says and give him what he wants, and a way of speaking that people (especially women) love to listen to.

He also has a great memory, which he formerly used to keep track of his products, deals, profits, debts and bets. He never had to write anything down and was very successful at his game – until he got busted.

In the quiet of his new cell he lays his eye upon the Bible in the corner. He begins reading and memorizing the Good Book, chapter and verse. There's no rush really; he has years to accomplish this task, and to shore up his jail house studies with historical information and sermons found with Google during his library time.

Our future pastor, a product of San Quentin, Attica or some other penitentiary will come out of prison with his Religious Pimp Game tight as hell.

While locked up, Quentin Attica starts to lecture on God and Jesus to the other convicts. He says the blessing at mealtime, and leads a group of convicts in Bible study on Tuesday and Thursdays in a corner of the yard. This serves as his internship.

All he has to do is explain that yes, he was all those horrible things before, but now he has seen THE LIGHT! The Lord "touched" him during his darkest hour while he was in prison, you see. Or maybe Jesus even spoke to him, or an Angel came in the dark in his cell. Whatever is his version of the story, somehow it involves an amazing transformation and contact with God or one of his representatives while behind bars.

When he is paroled from prison he starts giving sermons on street corners and in halfway houses. People start giving him money for making them feel better.

Pretty soon he becomes a familiar face, and people start trusting him. He begins talking to other people about starting a church. Some of them are regular trusting people, but many of them are his ex-buddies that are just as shady as he is... er WAS. They plan to serve as deacons and elders of his new non-denominational church.

One of them just happens to know of an old building they can rent cheap. They form a church with Quentin Attica at the helm, since he is the mouthpiece.

They spread the word far and wide of this exciting new, good-looking and single pastor. Women, hungry for the attentions of a new man and the promise of a better life, flock to him to soak up his energy and presence. Some married people may come too because they've heard this guy was touched and gives inspiring sermons.

None of them realizes that drug dealers and pimps, fences and gang leaders are some of the smoothest, most manipulative salesmen in the world, and they can easily create a feeling of "inspiration" whenever they want.

When Quentin Attica starts referring to himself as "doctor" he is legitimized even more, though he never even graduated from high school and his degree from the School of Hard Knocks with a Major in Gaming Women certainly provides him with no scholarly knowledge.

However, this guy is extremely smart and very driven (these are the same skills that made him successful in his bookie/pimp/drug-dealing business).

Week after week, month after month, more people come and fill the collection plate at Quentin Attica's new church. These people join the church and start tithing 10 percent of their gross salary as they have been instructed to do by God, so Quentin tells them.

They organize committees to start fellowshipping and having fried fish, sweet potato pie, and soul food dinner sales to bring in MORE people and MORE money.

Week after week, month after month, the needy, the broken, the confused, the lonely, and the desperate come and fill the collection plate. They're hoping for a miracle, a blessing, a break and some of the prosperity they've been promised if they give and their hearts are pure. If they have a job, they start tithing too.

Fast forward five years. Quentin Attica now heads up one of the largest churches in the area. He is a political and spiritual force to be reckoned with!

Quentin Attica, the very eligible bachelor, drives his silver gray Mercedes Benz SL drop top through the city on his way to his church, having left his million dollar estate in a gated community in the suburbs. He has the look of a sexually satisfied man, having recently returned from his romantic honeymoon in Europe.

After sleeping with half the parishioners of his church, he went to another city and brought back a wife. Furious at the betrayal but feeling guilty about having fornicated anyway, the women in his church stay quiet and deal with the disappointment of not being chosen to be First Lady.

They watch as his new wife, the Queen of the Quentin Attica Fiefdom takes her rightful place as his "helpmeet." She is rewarded for her support by being able to shop at only the finest stores. She wears fancy hats, suits, jewelry and furs in the winter. The Parishioners proudly point to the designer shoes and custom-made suits their good looking pastor wears. They find it exciting that their service and money made this man what he is today.

To reward his minions for their loyalty, he actually sits on a throne in the pulpit and puts on a great show every Sunday for their benefit. After all, they paid for the entertainment. And what a show it is! You can practically see the fire and brimstone rising up from the depths of hell as he sweats and paces and stirs the flock of sexually frustrated and lonely single women into an orgasmic frenzy!

"YES LAWD! THANK YOU JESUS! I LOVE YOU PASTOR!"

A decade later Doctor Quentin Attica is looking in the mirror at himself as he prepares for Sunday service. At 46 he is a well kept man with slightly graying temples and smooth brown skin, draped attractively in gold jewelry of the finest quality.

A quick look at his Cartier watch reminds him that it's time to go. As he slides on his fine Armani jacket, Quentin looks around at his 4500 square foot home and takes a moment to reflect back on the pimpin, rock slinging and five year incarceration that brought him to this moment.

He says to himself with a sly smirk *"Jesus really has been good for me."*

In 1972 the movie MARJOE won an academy award for best documentary feature. The film starred Marjoe Gortner, a tent revivalist that traveled the United States whipping people into a religious frenzy. The film's tagline: "You Keep the Faith...Marjoe Keeps the Money" was quite telling. Gortner started his career in childhood, so by the time the film was made he was an absolute master at getting people fired up and getting them to give him ridiculous amounts of cash in the name of Jesus. Then he and his family would fold up their tents, load up their trucks, go to the next town and do the same thing all over again.

As the documentary crew followed them from town to town in 1969/1970, Marjoe shared the tricks of his trade and how the con game of evangelism worked. Throughout the film he was breaking it down point by point. Fascinating stuff that you should see, as it will definitely open your eyes to the fire and brimstone, shouting and dancing, sing–song cadence and heart pounding music we see and hear in televangelists and mega churches today. Absolutely nothing about the basics of the con game of religion and church has changed in 50 years.

"My aunt has recently returned to a church she used to go to when she was a child. They now have a younger preacher who decided to remodel the church right in the middle of winter. He immediately started asking for more tithes and offerings, and kept trying to be slick by asking my aunt what she gets on her retirement check, do you own your own home, car etc. My aunt knows the drill and sidestepped his questions with questions of her own.

"Anyway, this fool tore down half the church while encouraging members to feel free to donate $1000 offerings. Those old people looked at him like he was crazy. Of course his friends were doing all the work on the church with no real contract, no board approval or anything. He put in chairs instead of pews (excuse me, our asses are meant for pews), and was remodeling his own house or had just bought one which was probably where the money was really going anyhow.

"The church had no heat for two weeks in January while this fool was trying to be slick about getting the heat back on with some offerings shit. My aunt stayed home!" ~Crystal G.

Be wary of the church you attend. Going to the wrong church will make you a sheep, blindly following the mandates of a small group of men you have placed in your life in a position of power. Going to the wrong church will make you malleable and predictable, and narrow your thinking, which thus limits your options. Going to the wrong church will put you in the position of being fleeced like a lamb by men who are there to prey on your neediness, your fears and your feminine emotional desires.

7

PULPIT PIMPS AND CONGREGATION HOS

The parallels between the street pimp's games of mental manipulation and the man in the pulpit's games of emotional control

Religion is regarded by the common people as true, by the wise as false, and by the rulers as useful. ~ Seneca (4 BC – 65 AD)

P.I.M.P. Means Put it in My Pocket

Many people find solace in church, a calming of their spirit, fellowship and understanding. They also enjoy being around people that they believe have a similar mindset and are attending services for the same reasons they are.

In reality, church is about getting and giving money, and the perceived power and benefits afforded from the exchange of said money. Churchianity is just like any other business that provides a "feel good" service in exchange for payment.

The style of preaching favored by black pastors begins with a deep, rich voice with a wide range of tonal qualities that they use like a wind instrument. Black church-goers rate their pastors message as "excellent" when he stirs their emotions by using a combination of chanting, melodious speech patterns, and call-and-response preaching during the service. Up and down, up and down, shouting then whispering. When delivering the "message" they follow the musical composer's rules of melody, rhythm and tone. The volume and cadence of a good preacher's words is hypnotic. Short phrases are repeated throughout the sermon for extra emphasis, designed to elicit a specific emotional and physical response from the congregation.

Evans Crawford, author of *The Hum: Call and Response in African American Preaching*, sets out five progressive affirmations to instruct the preacher through a powerful and motivating sermon presentation:

1. Help 'em Lord!

2. Well?

3. That's All Right!

4. Amen!

5. Glory Hallelujah!

The call and response method involves the listeners (the congregation), and often has them standing on their feet, raising their hands and faces up to God in appreciation as they answer or respond to questions posed by the preacher.

One morning, I heard the voice of Jesus saying, 'C'mon unto me and lay your burdens down! What did I do? I came to Jesus, just as I was. And I found in him joy in sorrow. Somebody shout yes. Yeesssss! I can't hear you talking to me! What you say? Yesssssssss Lord!

Observing videos of black preachers delivering sermons from all across the country in this style is easy to do on You Tube. The phrases, the singing, the jumping around, two-step buck dancing, the humming and the theatrical entreaties for God to save the sinners are the same from video to video. This "whoopin' and hollerin'" style of preaching, along with the congregation's unquestioning dependency upon their pastor to interpret the word of Almighty God for them has not changed since slavery.

Jeremiah Camara, author of *Holy Lockdown* remarked that he found the sermons of preachers across the nation to have a redundant sameness, sometimes delivered in a more impassioned manner, but still, the sermons had the familiarity of television reruns.

"Church rhetoric can sound like a broken record. It is apparent that preachers quite naturally run out of things to preach about, and are severely limited in terms of introducing us to more progressive and stimulating doctrines. (p.35) "The church, as with any other business, understands that familiarity breeds confidence. Preachers stick to rhetoric they know will produce 'Amens.' These are bread and butter Scriptures, phrases or popular clichés that preachers throw in their sermon soup, which are known for getting emotional and affirmative reactions from congregations. Repetition is the anchor of the black preacher's sermonic repertoire. Their survival depends on it." (p. 36)

Around the nation, black churches are filled primarily with women, and generally led by men. The women give the money and the men have the power; women give the time and men reap the benefits. The dishonesty in the business exchange is that the women feel good, but receive nothing tangible and go home with no evidence of a service being provided. It's a magician's illusion and a sleight of hand trick.

Even when I was very young, I understood that the pimp game has three sides – pimp, trick and ho, but there is just one winner in the game – the pimp. Several popular books about street pimping have been published over the past few years, including *Pimpology* by Pimpin' Ken, *Rosebudd: The American Pimp* by John Dickson, *The Pimp Game: Instruction Guide* by Mickey Royal, and Iceberg Slim's *Pimp: The Story of My Life*. One that I have in my personal library of collectible hardbacks has been out of print for decades. Published in 1972 *Black Players: The Secret*

World of Black Pimps absolutely fascinated me as an adolescent, and helped familiarize me with the games men use on women.

Reviewing books about the pimp life, one cannot help but notice the marked similarity between how street pimps from the 1960s/1970s recruited a female for prostitution, and how pulpit pimps recruit women in churches to manipulate them into giving him their money. Over the past 50-60 years, the pimp and 'ho game hasn't changed much. I suppose it really hasn't needed to because black women are still naive, still needy for male validation, and still led like lambs to slaughter by men with bright smiles, fast talk and tight game.

Big Pimpin' - The 10 Step Plan to Turning a Bitch Out

Pimps at the top of their game are masters at getting into the minds of females. The pimp's ability to get into the head of beautiful but not very bright women and stay there could mean the difference between having $2-3,000 in his pocket or building an empire of $2-3 million on the backs of women.

To become a great in the pimp game requires intelligence, a focus on getting what you want from everyone you come into contact with, and innate business acumen. The goal for the smart pimp is to use pimping as a stepping stone to entrepreneurial legitimacy, which is achieved by taking the money he earns from 'hoing, and quickly converting it into a thriving company.

> "Women give and give, but none of the tithing women get the deed to the church house. They don't own it. A congregation in my city had spent years raising money for the 'building fund.' Passa made the

congregation mad for some reason. They tried to fire him. He said 'OK!' Then he evicted the church. Apparently he had the deed and it never dawned on anybody to check whose name was on it." ~Angela M.

The smartest pimps seek to invest in credible enterprises such as real estate, the entertainment/recording industry or, of course, a church as soon as possible. No matter which industry the pimp ultimately selects, it all begins with successful recruitment and management of a group of women that he pimps. The women earn the money and then give it to the pimp. The basics on how-to flip a woman into "hoing" follows a pretty standard 10-step plan.

#1 Pimps look for those that are easily victimized – young teens in need of a friend to care for them, and broken souls. These girls are often runaways that the kindly, benevolent pimp finds arriving in a new city at bus terminals and train stations. There is a strong correlation between girls entering prostitution and various forms of child abuse – including sexual, physical and emotional. Experts report a surprisingly high percentage of prostitutes were victims of incest, rape, beatings, domestic violence, neglect and other related problems of family dysfunction. *Women that are wounded, depressed and carrying emotional baggage from abuse in childhood or economic and emotional stresses of broken relationships flock to churches. The women are there seeking spiritual comfort and support from a kindly, benevolent pastor.*

#2 Pimps zero in on those that look vulnerable, scared, troubled, confused, and hungry for something. The neediness is in their eyes. The pimp's game is to play the role of Fairy Godfather; he promises to provide support love and understanding, and to make all her dreams come true. Just like a drug dealer, a pimp never tells you the bad things they're going to do; instead they sell you a dream by telling you all the good things you want to hear. *James Warren Jones, better known as Rev. Jim Jones, founded The People's Temple in the 1950s. He gave himself the power to arrange and dissolve marriages at will, taking the women he wanted into his personal harem. Members were coerced into signing away money, property, artwork and inheritances to the People's Temple to the tune of hundreds of millions of dollars under the guise that they didn't need it. Their Fairy Godfather Jim Jones would take care of them and their every need. In the 1970s Jones took a large group to Guyana and formed Jonestown. When people had the gall to want to leave the compound with a visiting Congressman, Leo Ryan -- along with three members of the press that accompanied him -- were gunned down by Jones' henchmen. Subsequently, more than 900 Temple followers (most of them being black) were either injected with poison or drank poison Kool-Aid in a mass murder/suicide. Jim Jones also killed himself.*

#3 Pimps seek out the easy targets – lonely people that exhibit low self esteem. Most are overweight, insecure and not especially attractive or sexy. A pimp's victim may have limited social skills and lack street smarts or experience with men. *Many of the women that come to church seeking solace and comfort are grossly obese or have severe emotional problems best addressed by a psychotherapist. I believe problems from childhood sexual or physical abuse are often at the core of women's problems with obesity and a damaged sense of self. Depression/anxiety, addictions, and other mental/emotional illnesses should be treated with drugs and counseling. A woman with emotional problems is a sitting duck for unscrupulous church leaders and members. She needs professional help, not prayer or to be victimized further with sexual or financial manipulation.*

"At 24 I was newly married. This my first experience active in the Christian faith, and I was sexually assaulted and molested by the pastor. I went to him for 'counseling' as I was experiencing problems on the job and was beginning to have difficulty in my marriage. Finances were an issue as I worked to support my husband's desires for 'independence' and his business ventures. This made my job all the more crucial to sustain us financially. I was also coming to see the impact of the family dynamic of alcoholism in my life and personality and ability to emotionally protect myself in more complex relationships as an adult.

"For the first time ever, I shared my early experiences of molestation and rape during the first meeting with pastor. At the end of the session, he moved to hug me and proceeded to kiss me in the mouth and with his tongue. I do as victims of sexual abuse do, froze. I spoke the words, 'this is not right' and his response was something to the effect that God/Jesus understood and would forgive.

"I was able to let him know via body language I was not interested in this and he did not push further. He suggested we meet again. However, I told my husband what happened. Given my husbands history of early childhood adversity, he was unable to protect me and besides, this was HIS PASTOR from childhood as I joined this church he had been a member of for years.

"My husband and I went to meet with the pastor and he became anxious upon learning the reason. It was my intent to have him take responsibility for what he did to me. His first move was to have us 'schedule' an appointment. He was concerned that other members would hear, so we went back a night or two later. No other members where aware as I told no one else. Pastor took us into the main sanctuary away from the secretary and others who may overhear outside his door. This is when he acknowledged doing wrong and offered me the name and number of a 'professional' as I needed help. My husband took the number and I think at that moment I knew he and I would not last much longer.

"Pastor was eventually divorced from his wife following a sex scandal involving one of the older women in the church. It exposed his propensity toward sexual impropriety in the church and using his position to do so.

"Not long after, we stopped attending. I was introduced to crack-cocaine and my marriage broke up. I did not stay using long, six months to be exact, and I did seek professional help on my own. I have never looked back, having used the resource to get to know self and became a professional clinician myself. I have heard many stories of sexual, verbal and other forms of abuse perpetrated in the church and by members in high positions over the years." ~ Veronica A.

#4 After she is in the pimp's clutches, the next step is to get her totally dependent on him. He will tell her what to wear, what to think, what she can and cannot do by his standards – he basically owns her mind body and soul. *Pastors of some Pentecostal Holiness and Fundamentalist Christian churches are notorious for mandating that women wear dresses only and no "adornments" such as jewelry or makeup. It is not uncommon for churches to advise their members that even their own family should be shunned as being "of the world" and a bad influence. Such mandates effectively isolate the woman, making her world smaller and smaller as her socialization is limited to people within the church who are also under the pastor's rule. She is now totally dependent upon him as he guides her thoughts about herself and others, her behavior, and her attire. He has full control.*

> "I know a church where married and single women are having affairs with the trustees, and it is well known throughout the congregation. I have even been in church and the pastor was served for a divorce while he was preaching because he got one of the ushers pregnant! My ex-wife of 18 years was included with the garbage. I can no longer tell my teenage boys that church is a great place for spiritual growth, or that you can find a nice wife in church!" ~ Jason B.

#5 Pimps use legitimate job titles to draw women to them with promises of fame and fortune. Pimps are usually very intelligent and creative guys, and have been known to recruit women under the guise of being modeling agents, music video or film producers, photographers, rap artists, or recording industry A&R. *Young girls with stars in their eyes often fall prey to these legitimate-sounding careers. For a religious black woman, the ultimate fantasy man is one who sits at the right hand of God, a pastor or minister. Pastors, just like pimps are persuasive and charming. Since most women are highly auditory, a pimp's verbal skills quickly win a woman's interest, adoration and loyalty as he smoothly brings her into the stable with his "rap". Before she knows it, she is giving him her all as she hangs onto his every word. In church or on the street, a woman caught up with a pimp believes that if she just does what he says and devotes her time and money as he's told her to, all that he promises will become true.*

#6 Pimps promise the glamorous lifestyle. Pimps recruit runaways and girls in need of basic comforts such as food, shelter and affection. They promise lavish trips, cars, furs and jewelry and if she just does the things he says, this magic can happen for her. Girls that grew up without much in the way of food, nice clothes and shoes like other girls are vulnerable to promises of material things they've never had. *Coerced into believing that giving your pastor's church 10 percent of your income will mean you are blessed with health, wealth and comfort, you are likely to believe that prosperity and the lifestyle you dream of having will become available to you because of this man.*

#7 Pimps use other females to recruit new women. Stories are all over the web of young women befriending teen girls then inviting them to "parties" where the girls end up drugged, raped and forced into prostitution by someone they thought was a trustworthy friend. *Pastors instruct their parishioners to spread the word and bring new members into the church. When a woman meets a new man, one of the first things she is requested to do is to bring him to church with her to meet her pastor. Attractive new women that wander into the church often catch the eye of the pastor or other high level male in the church who makes it his business to befriend her with the ultimate goal of bedding her using any number of tricks and lies. The setup to betray her trust begins almost immediately upon meeting her.*

"On April 3, 2012, in Chesterfield, Virginia Kelvin Goode, a man who represented himself to church leaders as a minister was accused of trying to have sex with a 14-year old female member of the church. Goode allegedly met the girl at the Lord's Church Baptist in Chesterfield County and gave her a business card saying that he could 'help her' because she was 'in trouble.' The girl called to see what trouble she was in, and that's when the drama began. The girl's parents said Goode called their daughter multiple times after that, making sordid requests and asking inappropriate questions like whether she was a virgin. He solicited her to sleep with him, promising that he would pay for her college apartment and a car. He then tried to cover up his crime by requesting that she lie to her parents and say he was tutoring her. The girl's parents took out an order of protection against Goode, who it was discovered had eight felony convictions, primarily for domestic violence."

#8 A true pimp must keep his 'ho's under his control at all times. This goal is best accomplished by vigilantly guiding her every move and all of her choices. If she prefers someone or something more than you, it means your pimp game is weak. In the ideal pimp set-up, each and every move the 'ho makes must ultimately be for the pimp's benefit. She must see her pimp as the most important thing in both his life and hers. *"Instead of encouraging members of their church to seek out the word of God by reading their Bibles on their own, pastors teach their congregation to rely on them instead. They disguise this control by saying God has placed them in charge of their members, and that they only want the best spiritual success for their members, but that is simply not the truth. A proper church leader that really wants the best for the members in their church will give advice when asked according to what is written in God's word and not their own personal opinion. I have met several pastors that went so far as to tell people who they could date and who they couldn't. One pastor said 'I don't let girls in my church date or marry any boys unless they go to my church and I know them and approve them.' " ~ Rev. Johnny Lee Clary*

#9 The pimp relies on two key emotions to manipulate and control his 'hos – fear and love. A woman under the spell of a pimp believes that he truly cares about her and has her best interests at heart. If there is no man in her life, the pimp will become her substitute lover, brother, father, protector and provider. She often imagines that she is in love with him and that her feelings are returned; therefore, she'll do anything for him. *Church going single black women are notorious for saying that they are married to God or Jesus and don't need a human being for a man, or that they love their pastor, even if he has a wife. It is impossible for a man of flesh to meet the standards of a perfect God or Jesus Christ, so no regular fellow has a chance with these women. When a beloved pastor is accused of wrongdoing, the women of his church surround and protect him with all they have as if HE were God.*

#10 Pimps use a combination of seduction and terrorism to recruit and keep their 'hos. The pimp is alternately sweet and loving, then threatening and violently abusive. Whether the violence is real or merely threatened ("if you don't do it I will…"), the ho is in fear of not submitting to the demands of her pimp. He tightens his grip on her until she is totally dependent emotionally, physically and spiritually. Her history of dysfunctional familial or romantic relationships makes it easy for her to succumb to the 10 popular pimping techniques set out above. *Men's egos demand that they be right all the time, and to be right that means women must be wrong. Scripture is used to reinforce negative beliefs of women as emotional and weak while men are portrayed as logical and strong. Women are threatened with being single, unloved, labeled negatively by the church or of going to Hell. Men want to have the power and control, and to have power and control exclusively they must make sure that women have none. Once a woman's mind is wrapped up in church doctrine, the mental trap has been snapped shut and she's done.*

Using the 10 tactics outlined above, pimps convince women to prostitute their bodies in "sex for money" transactions. The properly trained ho will do almost anything to stay connected to her pimp and get his smiling approval. Once she is at that point, he has successfully "turned her out" and secured a steady source of income for as long as her health holds up and she stays out of jail. With a church woman, the pastor has secured a steady source of income for as long as her bank account holds up, and she stays out of the influence of a man who is not in his church.

Pastors are Mack Pimps

According to Joan J. Johnson, the author of a book entitled *Teen Prostitution*, the most successful type of pimp is what she refers to as "The Mack Pimp." Mack pimps are ranked as the elite class of pimps and usually have a much greater number of ponies in their stable than the entry-level player, or what she calls the tennis shoe pimp.

The Mack Pimp combines street smarts with sharp business acumen. Most Mack pimps usually invest their hoing money in a business and live a very comfortable middle-class lifestyle, often keeping a low profile in suburban bedroom communities. From all appearances, the Mack pimp living in the suburbs, driving a Range Rover or American made SUV is just a regular family guy.

Females can also be Mack Pimps, as several black women have moved into the front line of the religious pimp game. Look

157

at Prophetess Juanita Bynum for example (don't you just love these titles?)

With no formal training in theology, Juanita Bynum rose to fame in the late 1990s after tying her string to the coattail of one of the big names in the religious pimp game, T. D. Jakes. She is not a graduate of divinity school nor of any other college or university. Prior to getting the "calling" she worked as a hairdresser and a flight attendant for Pan Am.

In 2002, the Prophetess married Pastor Thomas Wesley Weeks III. It's said that she gave the 40 women attendants in her wedding diamond tennis bracelets for gifts, and that her wedding gown was embroidered with real Swarovski crystals. This ostentatious wedding fit for royalty was reported to have a $1.2 million price tag. When you think about what a church leader is supposed to represent to a community of middle- and lower-class working people, where does such expenditure on a wedding make sense? What kind of benefits could have been provided to children and single moms to get up on their education or career with that money? What kind of sports programs could have been started to get teens off the streets with that money? What could have been done more sensibly to help a black community with $1.2 million dollars?

There is no discernable difference between the Mack Pimp and the leader of any large, black, inner-city or mega church. They both live a nice lifestyle off the efforts of women; they both live middle-class lifestyles from the money other people give them from their work; they both use the pimp game to portray themselves as legitimate businessmen and community leaders;

and they both seek to control the minds of groups of women with the goal of using them for all they have.

8

SEXUAL PREDATORS AND PREY IN BLACK CHURCHES

Dangers lurk for children and women in church; when women and children are overly trusting of people they meet in church, bad things happen

Without game, men prey on each other.
~Perry Farrell

Pedophiles as Church Leaders

We live in a society that guides not only our own behavior, but also the behavior of parents, educators, and religious leaders. Our society is constructed around both man-made and spiritual laws, and all must be considered when assessing someone's true guilt or innocence. Black women are notorious for placing blind and unwavering faith in men they associate with, but when single moms are overly trusting in men and their churches, bad things happen to children.

Normal, heterosexual men do not concern themselves with other men's sex lives – they are too worried about their own. Religious and political leaders that blast homosexuality at every opportunity should be considered suspect. I've noticed that each high profile man that talked the most trash about gayness has turned out to be gay and exposed themselves as hypocrites.

Bishop Eddie Long presented himself as a spiritual leader, a surrogate father figure and a trusted man of God to the members of his congregation and the community. By involving himself in the homosexual sexual abuse of teens placed in his care by their trusting parents, Bishop Long violated every moral and spiritual law there is. Bishop Eddie Long also railed against homosexuality and same-sex marriage in sermon after sermon, even organizing a march in Atlanta which he called "Re-ignite the Legacy." The 2004 march against homosexuality and other ills of society attracted an estimated 25,000 people. With MLK's youngest daughter Bernice King by his side, Eddie Long attempted to walk his taste for boy-meat right out of his system. Too bad it didn't work.

It's become common to hear stories of pastors abusing their power over both women and children. Narcissistic and drunk with the deference shown them by church members and community leaders, these men come to believe they are invincible and able to get away with pretty much anything. They feel justified to take whatever they want financially, emotionally or physically from anyone vulnerable to their authority and charisma.

> "When I was 13, my choir went to another state to sing. While sitting in the back row, my pastor came back to where I was and whispered in my ear, 'You look good, I bet you taste good too!' I never went back to that church. He was single and what upset me the most was his 10-year-old son was sitting right near him when he did that. I have a little brother myself and I still remember the hurt on his son's face when he heard what his father said to me." ~ Tasha W.

Biblical Scriptures are frequently used by evil men as a tool to coerce others into doing their bidding. Their leadership position and the word of God are combined into a powerful potion that is used to manipulate impressionable mothers and children. Many black church leaders display a startling sense of entitlement to the resources and even the bodies of their congregants. Single and married women, trusting that the people they meet in church will be of good moral fiber, flock to churches in droves and take their children with them. The crimes set out below were committed by individuals that chose to prey on children because they know that Christian women and their children are easy targets.

Here are just a few examples of men heading up black churches around the country and how they forced or coerced minor children into illicit sexual activity and/or criminal acts:

- Mobile, Alabama, evangelist Anthony Hopkins, 39, was sentenced in May 2010 to life plus 51 years in prison after being convicted of killing his wife and storing her body in a home freezer. He received the legal maximum for the murder, and additional time for convictions of sexual abuse and sodomy of a child. Assistant District Attorney Ashley Rich called Hopkins "evil of the worst kind." She said he taught the eight children in his home things about the Bible that were not true and that helped him get away with his crimes for years. During Hopkins' trial in April, prosecutors said he killed his 36-year-old wife, Arletha Hopkins, in 2004 after she caught him molesting a girl, then stuffed her body in a freezer at their home. Investigators discovered the body in 2008 after a young woman abused by Hopkins told child advocates about the assaults.
- Rev. William Bosley of Kenosha, Wisconsin, was sentenced to 55 years in prison for sexually abusing a six-year-old girl in his church while her blind mother was cleaning the building. He also pleaded guilty to sexually abusing the child's 12-year-old sister in the home of their grandmother. The sentencing took into account Bosley's recent conviction for firing a gun into a car and the fact that he had served a 28-month sentence for sexual abuse of an 11-year-old girl in Washington state 20 years before.
- Polk County Sheriff's Office Special Victims detectives arrested two volunteer ministers at an Auburndale church after a 12-year-old girl reported the men, whom she met at the church, had sexually abused her during the summer of 2011. Minister Clevon Ghent, 35, was charged with five counts of custodial

sexual battery. His nephew, Gernard Jones, 18, was charged with three counts of lewd battery for his participation in the multiple rapes. The girl was a member of the church congregation.

• Apostle Gerald Fitroy Griffith was convicted in Maryland's Howard County Circuit Court in 1997 of sexually assaulting a 15-year-old boy that said he once viewed Griffith as a father figure. Griffith was the founding pastor of Redemption Christian Fellowship Church in Gwynn Oak, Maryland. He was facing charges of assaulting five more boys when he copped a plea and accepted a 15-year sentence in prison.

• North Las Vegas police arrested Pastor Billy Eckstine McCurdy, aged 57, following an eight-month investigation into allegations that he sexually assaulted teen boys at his home. McCurdy was the pastor at Revival Temple Church of God in Christ in Vegas. This arrest occurred five years after similar charges against him were dropped. The new charges involved two teen boys who said McCurdy forced them into sexual relationships with him. They told police he used his position in the church and Bible Scriptures to force them into sex acts.

• A North Carolina minister was arrested in August 2010 on charges he had sex with a minor child 14 years of age. Darryl Todd, the 32-year-old senior pastor of Spring Branch Missionary Baptist Church in Wagram was charged with three counts of statuary rape according to arrest warrants. All three incidents occurred in April and May 2010, according to police.

• A prominent Harlem pastor resigned in September 2010 amid charges by a retired NYPD cop and nine other men that he molested them when they were children. Monsignor Wallace Harris was the highest-ranking black cleric in the archdiocese and once considered for appointment as a bishop.

• A 51-year-old Washington state pastor was sentenced in 2010 to 18 years in prison after pleading guilty to raping and molesting a boy multiple times over a six-year period beginning when he was just 9 years old. Pastor James Watkins' sentence was at the top of the range for his conviction on three counts of child rape and one count of child molestation. Watkins was arrested and charged after the victim came forward out of concern that Watkins was grooming another victim.

- A local pastor accused of fathering the child of a 13-year-old member of his congregation has been formally indicted by a Bowie County grand jury for aggravated sexual assault of a child. Willie Fay Arnold, 60, is accused of sexually assaulting the child in her grandmother's residence in Texarkana, Texas.

- Bishop Robert Reaves, a former minister at Cedar International Fellowship in Durham, North Carolina, was found guilty of first-degree murder and sentenced to life in prison without the possibility of parole for the murder of the girlfriend of a young man he wanted sexually. Bishop Reaves, a closeted homosexual with an anti-gay agenda, made "unsuccessful advances toward other male friends and [also] took revenge on their girlfriends." Prior to this conviction, Reaves had twice been charged with sexual misconduct with young boys.

- A pastor faces at least 25 years in prison after being convicted of aggravated sexual battery and child molestation of his 15-year-old foster child, authorities said. DeKalb County prosecutors contend Bishop Frederick Kelley, who headed Greater New Macedonia Church of God in Christ in Decatur, Georgia, had a history of child molestation and rape involving family members going back 35 years.

- Jerry Darnell Bartley, 39, was charged with six counts of sodomy and one count each of second-degree child abuse, sex abuse of a minor, sex abuse of a minor continuing course of conduct and second-degree assault. Police documents show that Bartley was a licensed foster parent and served as pastor at the

Faith and Deliverance Church in Chestertown, Maryland at the time of his arrest. According to Kent County District Court documents, Bartley sexually abused a 13-year-old boy numerous times between Christmas 2009 and April 5, 2010. A medical examination by the Talbot County Children's Advocacy Center found that the boy had injuries consistent with being sexually abused. Bartley is accused of sexual abuse so severe as to cause the boy internal injuries.

- A pastor charged with sexually abusing children said his congregation is supporting him and he has no plans to leave the church. Edwin House is accused of sexually abusing two 14-year-old girls in his home. His wife, Lovenia House is accused of failing to properly protect the children. After an attempted suicide in July 2010, the girl finally told a counselor that she was depressed after having been molested by Edwin House. She said the abuse started when she was 7, with the latest incident occurring when she was 9.

- In February 2012 Sacramento California pastor Cornelius Taylor was convicted on eight counts of sexual assault on a minor. A troubled teen with no family support was befriended by Taylor at his church. She moved in with the pastor and his wife when she was 16 years old. Taylor repeatedly sexually assaulted the girl in incidents that continued after she turned 18 years old. He faces a sentence of almost 8 years.

- Pastor Keith Pettis has completed nine months of his 20- to 24-year prison sentence after being convicted of child sex crimes against a foster child, alleging that he had sexually abused a 12-year-old girl in his home in August 2006 by performing a sex act on her. He allegedly sexually abused her again on Sept. 1, 2008, and Sept. 20, 2008, then forced her to perform a sex act on him in February and March of 2009. He was found guilty of nine counts that included taking indecent liberties with a child and sex offense of a child, among other charges. Despite his conviction and new residency at Central Prison in Raleigh, Pettis continues to have support from many people he ministered to at New Life Christian Center in Lowell, North Carolina, which includes a march and rally. His supporters believe the 12 year old lied and that their pastor didn't get a fair trial. "We forgive the brother but we're going to make them do the right thing," preached Pastor Boyd.

- Rev. Laneer D. Fisher, 39, was convicted by a Beaver County, Pennsylvania, jury in September 2011 of indecent assault, unlawful contact with a minor and corruption of a minor. Fisher was sentenced to serve six to 23½ months in jail, followed by three years' probation as a sexually violent predator. Fisher was found guilty of kissing and inappropriately touching a teenage boy who was a member of the church where Fisher was a pastor, Miracle Church of God in Christ. He faces a second trial, in Beaver Falls, Pennsylvania, for indecent assault, indecent exposure, corruption of minors and unlawful contact with a minor. In that case, police said Fisher also is accused of having illegal contact with a teenage boy.

- Keith James Boyd, a 44-year-old minister who had a three-month sexual relationship with a 16-year-old girl, has been convicted of two sex crimes by a St. Tammany, Louisiana parish jury. The married pastor of Open Door Apostolic Church in Slidell was convicted in March 2012 of carnal knowledge and indecent behavior with a juvenile. In Louisiana carnal knowledge is punishable by up to 10 years in prison and indecent behavior with a juvenile carries up to seven years imprisonment.

- Timothy Jackson, the 48-year-old former pastor of a Abundant Life Church in Detroit was sentenced in April 2012 to 40 years in prison for raping an 11-year-old member of his congregation. Jackson was found guilty of multiple counts of first-degree criminal sexual assault. Authorities say the girl was 11 when the sexual assaults began at the church, and continued between 2009 and 2010. The girl reported the rapes in August 2010.

- In April 2012, a Baltimore City Circuit Court jury found pastor Leon W. Jones guilty of sexually assaulting a 15-year-old girl from April 2000 until March 2002. The victim, now 27, was first introduced to Leon W. Jones by her mother, who also participated in the sexual abuse and pleaded guilty to five counts of sexual child abuse for her role. The jury found Jones, 61, guilty of eight counts of sexual offense in the second-degree. He faces a maximum of 160 years in prison and was scheduled to be sentenced in June 2012.

- In March 2012, Joseph Walker III, head pastor of one of Nashville's largest churches, Mt. Zion Baptist Church, is facing a total of five charges of sexual misconduct which reportedly took place over at least a 10-year period. All four women allege they were sexually exploited and abused during counseling sessions sponsored by the church, and that church leaders "regularly recruited women for exploitation and sex." He is also being sued by the husband of a woman who claims Walker's 'sexual misconduct with his wife broke up his marriage, causing him to have a nervous breakdown. A female minister-in-training witnessed the misconduct and brought it to the attention of church leaders. She reports that after doing so she became the victim of retaliation, stalking, and emotional and spiritual abuse. In response to the lawsuits the church released a statement which reads: "It is truly sad that a church and its leaders can be attacked with such shocking and ugly charges when the apparent motive is to extract huge sums of money from the congregation and its leaders."

- Dwayne "DJ" Wilson, 25, who worked at Greater St. Mark Church of God In Christ (COGIC) in Southwest Memphis as the church's "musical minister," was arrested Nov. 17. 2009 and charged with statutory rape involving a 16-year-old choir member. According to the girl's father, Wilson first became involved with the girl in February when she was 15 and singing in the choir. "There's so much sexual misconduct going on in COGIC right now, and he's right in the middle of it," the girl's father said. "It's out of control."

It's important to acknowledge that I am not blaming single mothers or black women for the behavior of pedophiles masquerading as honorable, God-fearing Christians. These are mature men in full control of themselves, with knowledge of the law, and the boundaries of appropriate behavior for adults in positions of authority.

I don't know any woman that would even think that their child would not be safe with their pastor, well-taken care of and treated with the same love and devotion she would provide. Sadly, as we've seen from the examples above, that is not always what happens.

> "...The final straw came when I found out that a convicted child molester was allowed to keep his position in the youth ministry, and I was called 'judgmental' and 'unforgiving' when I wouldn't allow my child to be anywhere near this man. He was a low-level offender on probation and the church knew about his past, but did nothing. Later, a woman who had foster children reported to CPS what was going on and the man was removed from his position and left the church soon after.

I wasn't the only person who didn't want a child molester 'teachin' their children anything! The realization that these fools really expected me to knowingly endanger my child in the name of God was what woke me up." ~Mary L.

With an estimated 75 percent of black children being raised in single-parent homes, most mothers raising sons without the child's father would welcome the opportunity for their son to be in the company of a trusted male like their pastor. I think it's perfectly normal for a single mom to be thrilled that her son was selected for a special program or recognition by her revered spiritual advisor -- a man she looks at with awe.

Many Christian women don't want to hear stories of depravity in religion. Instead of dealing with reality, Scriptures such as "Do not touch My anointed ones, And do My prophets no harm" (1Ch 16:22) are used to justify their unfaltering opposition to any criticism of their pastor's questionable behavior. These women prefer to pretend that such abhorrent crimes could never happen in THEIR church because THEIR church is attended only by solid Christian men of good faith and Godly behavior. THOSE other people weren't "real" Christians.

Well sistahs, think again! Statistics report that in 78 percent of sexual abuse cases, the victim or their family knows the perpetrator of the abuse. And churches are in actuality exactly where one is most likely to find such social misfits and sexual deviants. Since black people don't tend to believe in psychotherapy and counseling, where else would they go but church to seek assistance with quelling the fires of strange desire, their inner demons of sinful secrets and perverse fantasies about sex with children?

Youths Are at High Risk for Sexual Assault

In December 2011, a study spearheaded by the National Institute of Justice and the Department of Defense published its findings. The National Intimate Partner and Sexual Violence Study began in 2010 and included telephone interviews with a total of 16,507 adults nationwide.

The survey found that young people were at the greatest risk for sexual violence and assault. Some 28 percent of male victims of rape reported that they were first assaulted when they were less than 10 years old. Only 12 percent of female rape victims reported being assaulted when they were 10 or younger, but almost half of female victims said they had been raped before they turned 18. A full 80 percent of rape victims reported that they had been raped before age 25.

(These numbers are, I believe, not quite accurate due to the fact that my own research on female sexual assaults has alerted me to the fact that many young girls do not fully understand the behaviors that constitute sexual assault. They don't understand that coercion, even if they were convinced to say stop fighting after repeated pressure by a male, still constitutes a sexual assault. The first words out of her mouth were "no!" and she kept saying "no!" so whatever happens after that is rape.)

When it comes to recognizing a pedophile, many parents imagine him to be a trenchcoat-wearing sleaze bucket hanging around parks and playgrounds, easily picked out of the crowd. In reality, child molesting pedophiles lead amazingly normal lives, hiding their bizarre sexual attraction to children in plain sight. Think about the men you know and trust around your children -- relatives, neighbors, teachers, coaches, clergymen and police officers. Some of these respected family men are pedophiles.

> "Not saying all pastors are criminals but it's true some have ungodly pasts. I left one church were the pastor was caught on tape saying he loved to see the young boys dance on tables in the Atlanta clubs. He was being blackmailed by one of his male lovers who taped the phone conversation. It was scandalous and lots of folks lost faith in church all together after that scandal." ~Michaela E.

Black Christian women across the country were not overly concerned when stories of child sexual abuse surfaced in the Catholic church. The commonly expressed belief was that priests (being sexually frustrated from years of abstinence) were much more likely to sexual assault someone than a married protestant minister or pastor that had sex regularly with his wife.

On the surface that makes sense, but how do you explain the fact that in the U.S., 50 percent of pedophiles arrested for their crimes are married, most with families of their own? Keep in mind this figure represents only those that are actually caught.

The Predator's Game of Sexual Coercion

Law enforcement officials agree that the most underreported crime in the country is sexual assault, with more than 60 percent never reported to police at all. The thought that less than half of all cases of assault are reported is mind boggling, due to the fact that statistics estimate that "on average, 24 people per minute are victims of rape, physical violence, or stalking by an intimate partner in the United States. Over the course of a year, that equals more than 12 million women and men."

FBI statistics tell a very different story, however. In the United States, a rape is reported every five minutes. However, the FBI estimates that only about 16 percent of rapes are ever reported to the police. (FBI Uniform Crime Report, 1997)

A 1992 crime report sets out the following stats on sexual assault of females in the U.S. by age

>60 percent of the women who reported being raped were under 18 years old

>**29 percent were less than 11 years old**

>32 percent were between 11 and 17

>22 percent were between 18 and 24

>7 percent were between 25 and 29

>6 percent were older than 29

>3 percent age was not available

>(Rape in America study 1992)

In a survey of victims who did not report rape or attempted rape to the police, the following was found as to why no report was made: 43 percent thought nothing could be done, 27 percent felt it was a private matter, 12 percent were afraid of police response, and 12 percent felt it was not important enough. (Kilpatrick et al., 1992)

An article in the Boston Herald (May 2007/J. Heslam) reported that "clergy abuse in black churches of all denominations is vastly underreported, experts said, with young victims too terrified to come forward for fear of being blamed and banned from their close-knit, family-oriented houses of worship. It is much more widespread than any of us want to believe," said David Clohessy, the national director of the Chicago-based Survivors Network of those Abused by Priests. "All sexual abuse is underreported. We believe clergy sex abuse more than most and clergy sex abuse in the minority communities is even less reported."

Clohessy, who spent two years working in minority communities and churches in Boston, said it's much harder for minority victims to grasp that they will be believed and supported, not blamed due to the fact that minorities hold their religious leaders in even higher esteem; "The tendency of the church community is to gather around and protect the minister, almost to the point of blindness."

The power of the black pastor and the reverence with which parishioners hold him was exemplified in early 2012. Those in power at Christ Tabernacle Missionary Baptist Church in Jacksonville, Florida decided to ban children from attending Sunday services to protect their new pastor.

Several years ago Pastor Gilyard pled guilty to charges of lewd conduct and lewd molestation of two underage girls. (While he was the pastor of a different church Gilyard molested a 15-year-old girl and sent a lewd text message to another child.) Under the conditions of his plea agreement, Gilyard cannot have unsupervised contact with minors. The parishioners at his new church decided they'd rather have an admitted sex offender leading the congregation than have the children of the families that support the church attend services with their parents. Amazing.

> "You would think people would look at the corruption going on with these preachers and wake up, but some still won't. What kind of God would keep allowing a man who molested members of his congregation to be his representative? That's the dumbest shit ever!" ~Keith S.

Predators in the Pews

Though stories of ministers, pastors and priests molesting children are frequently reported in the news, the greatest threat to your child comes from other members of the church. Most parents are diligent about teaching their children not to talk to strangers; warnings about "stranger danger" are often frequent and detailed. However, parents in church are likely to relax their guard as they feel they are among trusted friends and that their children are safe.

Nothing could be further from the truth.

The term pedophilia encompasses a wide range of behaviors by the perpetrator: touching kids, fondling of genitals, exposing themselves to the child or requesting to see the child's genitalia, oral/genital contact, pornography and even kidnapping, rape and murder. Though sexual gratification is a component of pedophilia, psychologists report that the key motivator behind sexual abuse and rape is the power these men have over someone younger, weaker, trusting and naïve. In other words, naïve church-going women and their children are vulnerable to the sexual predators active in churches nationwide.

A landmark study was published by the University of Missouri-Columbia (April 2008) entitled *Entrapping the Innocent: Toward a Theory of Child Sexual Predators' Luring Communication*. According to the researchers, the first goal for the abuser is always to gain access to the potential victim and his or her family, and then to gain their trust.

Having the trust of the young person makes it much easier to coerce the victim into maintaining silence about the abuse as well. Children want to continue the friendship and feel responsible for maintaining the relationship by their silence. Many church-raised children are intentionally kept ignorant of the behaviors and activities that constitute sexual abuse, much to their detriment.

Single mothers and their naïve children are especially vulnerable because the friendly, engaging men met at church often show both parent and child the attention and affection they've been missing.

"Deceptive trust-building may be especially prevalent in relationships where the person has a position of authority over the child, such as a teacher or priest. Particular roles such as teacher or priest have an aura of respect, putting children in a position to obey their directions. Additionally, in society, these roles are often labeled as safe for children to seek out help or comfort. This results from the perception of the authority figure as a powerful and trustworthy figure in the child's life." (Lebacqz & Baron, 1991).

A majority of parents don't know nor understand the processes used by predators to prepare young people for sexual victimization. Those shocked that boys 15-17 years of age would fall prey to maneuvers attributed to Bishop Long have inevitably blamed the victims in some way, stating that they "must have been gay to begin with" or "they must have liked it" or "they asked for it!" For some reason, victim blaming in cases of sexual assault is a common and embarrassing mindset of many African Americans. I believe the mindset popular among blacks that "men only treat you the way you let them" is what fuels this shameful victim-blaming attitude.

Sexual abuse of any sort, but especially sexual exploitation of a child, constitutes an abuse of power - the older and physically stronger person takes advantage of a child for his sexual gratification. Typically, the adult possesses the power in the relationship, which leads the child to comply unquestioningly with the adult's requests (Abel, Becker, & Cunningham-Rathner, 1984). Men that laughed and joked about the plaintiffs in the Eddie Long case, saying that such things would never have happened to *them,* have little to no understanding of the wide variance with which children mature both physically and cognitively.

Since it's unlikely that a street-smart, teenage boy would be attending church anyway, those laughing the hardest would definitely not be on the hit list of a pedophile seeking a naïve, sheltered, emotionally needy teen. They didn't take into account that pedophiles are experts at finding children that are less emotionally developed, more vulnerable and thus more easily influenced. Sadly, yet importantly, many perpetrators have indicated during interviews that they are almost instinctively able to pick out a child that will make a good victim (Holmes & Slap, 1998).

Eddie Long's "Spiritual Sons" and their parents were of course appreciative of his offer to provide caring, guidance to their children. Imagine the pride a single mom would feel that her son was singled out by Bishop Long for participation in the Longfellow's Youth Academy! But what mother would not be alarmed if she knew that her son being plied with gifts and trips had a much more sinister motive?

Though I don't blame the mothers and children for anything to do with Bishop Long's behavior, I sometimes wonder how blinded by their religious beliefs black women can truly be and why they aren't more suspicious of men in churches.

There's a very revealing video of Eddie Long preaching a sermon based on Genesis 48:13-14. This dialogue is available for listening on You Tube in a video entitled Eddie Long Cranks Up a New Dance called Cross It Up (http://youtu.be/pTi2wjeyyBc). The video was recorded during a Sunday morning nightclub party at New Birth Missionary Baptist Church. Every time I see this video I am in awe of the almost hypnotic trance he is able to invoke over the more than 5,000 people attending the service.

In shock, I ask myself why don't they see the smirk on his face? Long can't even look at the crowd and keep a straight face, he has to look down and fumble with his sweat cloth to keep from bursting out laughing! Didn't they hear him call them "crazy people" right to their faces? Am I the only one that sees that this guy and his background singers view this entire thing as nothing but a Hollywood performance? And right in the middle of his show he struts across the pulpit stage asking no one in particular, "*Where my young people at? Where my Sporty's at? Where my little Shorty's at?*" He is focusing on young boys right in the middle of his presentation, as he jumps and chants like a hip-hop Hype Man during a service that is supposed to be about God's word.

Cognitive Brain Development in Teens

Though there are many highly intelligent teens with the ability to perform complex calculations and make inventive creations, most teen's ability to make decisions that require judgment can be shockingly poor. Research shows that cognitive maturity occurs in the mid-20s. As parents it is important that we not allow our children younger than 25 to make critical decisions without our input or guidance. The brains of teens and young adults have limited capacity for such abstract assessment of cause and effect. Young men and women well into college may still demonstrate difficulty with concepts such as:

- Mature judgment
- Seeing into the future
- Seeing how current behavior can affect the future
- Associating cause and long-term effect
- Moral intelligence
- Emotional intelligence
- Abstract thinking
- Seeing what is not obvious
- Planning and decision-making
- Rational behavior
- Understanding rules of social conduct

If you are the parent of an adolescent, teen or young adult under the age of 25, it is important that you heed this information and safeguard your offspring. Don't believe that because you sit down in a church and pray with hundreds or even thousands of people that you are all of a similar moral cloth and your children are safe from harm.

Remember, you don't know anything about the history or motivations of those running or attending churches. By being naive to the dangers of the situation, you place yourself in a very vulnerable position by trusting unknown people with your family's most valuable treasure – the health and happiness of your children. It's your job to protect and guide your babies until they are old enough to protect and guide themselves.

The Tricks of a Child Molester

What is sexual coercion? I believe it is best described as any behavior or use of pressure by one person designed to induce another to have undesired sexual or physical contact. Sexual coercion of children can include many other behaviors other than actual intercourse such as being pressured into kissing, caressing, heavy petting, oral sex, genital touching and any other undesired sexual behavior that makes the victim feel uncomfortable.

Coercive pressure to engage in unwanted sex acts may be applied to the victim, whether a child or an adult, verbally, physically or emotionally.

- **Physical pressure** can include hitting, kicking, pushing, pinching and slapping the victim into submission. Also included are forceful behaviors such as holding the victim down; blocking the victim from escaping a car, room or other enclosed space until they give in; continuing with the sexual behavior after the perpetrator has been told to stop (often repeatedly); and continuing to kiss or grope the victim as he/she tries to pull away or escape.
- **Verbal pressure** includes behaviors like threatening to use physical force against the victim; screaming at the victim; name calling; outright lying, or threats of blackmail ("if you don't do it I'll tell everyone you did anyway"). Harassment or badgering of the victim can include talking and phone calls, as well as high-tech methods such as sexually oriented text messages (sexting), voicemails, Twitter tweets, Facebook or

other social media stalking, or emails with inappropriate photo attachments.

- **Emotional pressure** is used much more frequently than physical and verbal pressure and is the most subtle of all the sexual coercion tactics. Using emotional pressure includes the perpetrator convincing the victim that he/she cares more for the victim than he/she actually does and will "take care" of them. Others may threaten to leave the victim and break off contact, triggering fears of abandonment. Repeated requests and pressure is another tactic often used, designed to wear the victim down until they give in to keep the peace or please the perpetrator to whom they have an emotional attachment. Guilt-tripping the victim by making them feel obligated to participate in sexual acts referencing "how nice I've been to you and your mom', utilizing peer pressure and even the perpetrator using his/her position of authority over the victim.

How Child Molesting Pedophiles 'Groom' Their Victims

Most parents perceive that child molesters are weird looking smelly men with thick glasses, suspenders and pot bellies that abduct children off the streets. The reality is that most children are molested not by strangers, but by someone they know and believe they can trust. Before the molestation actually occurs, the perpetrator puts his plan in motion to solidify a relationship with your child which helps reduce resistance. Most are very patient and can prep your child slowly and steadily over a period of many months.

The plan the child molesting pedophile utilizes sets the stage for a sexual assault on your baby. These behaviors are referred to by psychologists as "grooming" techniques. Grooming techniques are designed to gain the trust of not only the child victim, but also their trusting and often naïve parents. The child molester's plan is methodical and carried out with the greatest stealth, to intentionally mask any sign of an ulterior motive. The molester's goal is threefold:

(1) to gain unsupervised access to your child;

(2) to abuse the child for their own pleasure as frequently as possible; and

(3) to make sure the child keeps the abuse a secret for the rest of his or her life.

Acquaintance molesters are people that look like you and me. They're the people we think we know and trust to spend the night in our home, and to be in rooms and on trips and in cars alone with our children. They're pastors or priests, teachers, doctors, next-door neighbors, and mom's boyfriend or an old family friend of her dads. Acquaintance molesters often position themselves to become volunteers or employees of organizations or involved in professions that allow them to be in close proximity to children. Scouting organizations, youth after-school programs, sports coaches, teachers and youth church group volunteers are perfect examples of where acquaintance molesters like to hide out, waiting to prey on your children.

In his publication, "Child Molesters: A Behavioral Analysis," (http://www.missingkids.com/en_US/publications/NC70.pdf)

former FBI agent Kenneth V. Lanning lays out the grooming process:

> "Acquaintance child molesters typically groom and seduce their child victims with the most effective combination of attention, affection, kindness, privileges, recognition, gifts, alcohol, drugs, or money until they have lowered the victims' inhibitions and gained their cooperation and "consent." The skilled offender adjusts his methods to fit the targeted child. Offenders who prefer younger child victims are more likely to first "seduce" the victim's parents/guardians to gain their trust and obtain increased access to the potential victim. The offender then relies more on techniques involving fun, games, and play to manipulate younger children into sex. Those who prefer older child victims are more likely to take advantage of normal time away from their family and then rely more on techniques involving ease of sexual arousal, rebelliousness, inexperience, and curiosity to manipulate the children into sex.
>
> "Some offenders simultaneously befriend their victim's parents/guardians (e.g., telling parents/guardians they want to mentor or help their child) and work to alienate the child from the parents/guardians (e.g., telling children their parents/guardians don't want them to have fun)."

According to Lanning, the child molesting pedophile's grooming process has five distinct stages:

(1) gathering information about interests and vulnerabilities;

(2) gaining access (i.e., sports, religion, education, online computers);

(3) filling emotional and physical needs;

(4) lowering the child's inhibitions; and

(5) gaining and maintaining control (i.e., bonding, competition, challengers, peer pressure, sympathy, threats).

"Although the vulnerability may be greater when a troubled child from a dysfunctional family is groomed by an adult authority figure, the fact is any child can be groomed by any reasonably nice adult with interpersonal skills."

What to Do if You Suspect Sexual Abuse

Parents are often not aware their child is associating with a child molesting pedophile because the plan is so secretive and subtle. The well-practiced pro-level child molesters often groom multiple children simultaneously. These guys have plan A, B, and C working at the same time to cover their needs in case a child moves away, escapes from the grooming process through parental involvement, or turns out not to meet all their requirements. The child molester also keeps potential victims in various stages of grooming at all times so that they have ready replacements for the children whose bodies develop and change as they mature. Once the child is of an age where he or she no longer triggers his sexual fantasies, he moves on to the next, already prepped victim.

Parents must be more suspicious of the people that are around their children and know why they are there. This is especially important if someone shows an exceptional interest in your child – wanting to touch or kiss him/her, giving gifts for no reason, following them around at picnics or barbecues where there are large groups of people, showing undue attention that is not shown to other children, or finding reasons to be alone with your child (*i.e.,* offering to babysit).

If you suspect that your child is being groomed for molestation at a future date, intervene immediately. Let the pedophile know that you are aware of what is going on. Demand that they stay far away from your and any other child in your circle of protective influence or risk legal intervention and prosecution.

Should you suspect that your child has already fallen pretty to a child molester, or your child tells you that he or she has actually been abused, please follow these guidelines:

1. Stay calm. Fear and anger are normal parental reactions, but they can frighten your child. Be sure not to blame, punish, or embarrass the child. Remember, your child is an innocent victim.
2. Believe your child. It is very rare for a child to lie about sexual abuse. Many children who report abuse are not believed, especially if the identified abuser is a trusted family friend or relative. Do not deny or ignore what your child is telling you.
3. Listen to your child carefully. Take your child to a private place and let them tell you what happened in

his or her own words. Give your child your full attention and loving support.

4. Reassure your child that it wasn't their fault. Assure them that you are glad he or she told you. Give positive messages such as, "I know it's not your fault", or "I'm glad you told me." Be sure to let your child know they are not to blame.
5. Guard your child immediately from the accused abuser. Reassure the child that he or she is safe and that you will provide protection from any further pain.
6. Call 9-1-1 to report the suspected abuse immediately to your local police or sheriff, and/or Child Protective Services agency.
7. Do not confront the offender in your child's presence! In fact, it is probably best to let the proper authorities confront the offender, in case you cannot control your anger.
8. Seek medical help for your child as needed, along with professional mental health assistance with a counselor trained to treat child victims of sexual abuse and their family.
9. Use discretion and respect your child's privacy. Be careful not to discuss the abuse in front of or with people who do not need to know what happened.
10. Let your child talk about it in their own time. Don't pressure your child into talking about the abuse if they aren't ready to. Attempting to force information sharing can be traumatic, and you are not trained to interview a child sexual assault victim. On the other hand, do not try to silence your child. Allow your child to open up and talk, as they are comfortable.

11. Encourage your child to express his or her feelings, but keep your own feelings about the abuse separate. Do not make your child deal with his or her feelings as well as yours.
12. Try to resume as "normal" a life as possible. Protect your child, but don't make him or feel different or isolated or like they are being punished.
13. Don't dismiss your child's feelings by telling them to "forget about it" because "it was no big deal". You and your child will both need time to work through all the feelings and changes, especially if the offender is someone in the family. The time it takes for a child to heal varies, depending upon the child as well as the circumstances of the sexual assault (such as who the offender is, how long the abuse continued, whether or not threats, bribes, or force was used, and the type of abuse).
14. Be sure to seek help for yourself. Parents often feel angry, guilty, or to blame when they learn their child has been sexually assaulted – like they should have known or been there to protect the child. Talk to a good friend, someone you trust, or see a counselor.

Parents must be open and honest with their children about sexual molestation, and stop hiding behind the Bible or church to keep children ignorant. We live in a high tech, high pressure society; there are dangers for children everywhere you turn – educate yours about those dangers.

Your children are vulnerable and innocent. Their vulnerability gives the pedophile a great deal of influence over their chosen victims. Learn to recognize when your child may be threatened by a child molester in the grooming phase of attack.

Learning to recognize sexual coercion will help prevent your child from being irreparably harmed. Once your child is sexually abused, it cannot be undone and they never get their innocence back. You are the only one that can prevent that, and you must stop being so trusting of any and everyone just because they go to church.

Respect Your Little Person as an Individual

I also want parents to understand how something they do may be ultimately damaging to their child.

Too many times I've seen young children say "no!" and push away from an adult that wants a kiss or a hug. They don't want that person to touch them, pick them up, or kiss on them. Inevitably, the parents will force the child into allowing unwanted physical contact with this adult, which teaches a child that his or her body is not their own to control.

You may THINK that your order for your six-year-old boy to kiss and hug Uncle Frank is harmless, and that it's no big deal that Cousin John wants to sit your four-year old daughter on his lap and snuggle. But in the grand scheme of things, you are teaching your child to become a victim of a sexual predator by getting them accustomed to being ordered around by adults in situations where they must allow close physical contact and kisses, whether they want them or not. Bad move.

By refusing to allow children the right to control who touches them, and when, and where, parents are setting their children up for easy victimization by a pedophile. You are in this case coercing your own child into physical contact with someone they clearly do not want to touch their body, or whom they don't want to be close. Please stop this behavior immediately and respect your little person's right to control their own body.

Other suggestions for parents:

(1) Discuss drugs, alcohol and sexuality openly. Teach your children about their bodies, good touches, bad touches and which words said to them would be inappropriate and warrant telling Mommy and/or Daddy.

(2) Provide your children with a safe word so they know if this person really was sent by you to give them a message or pick them up.

(3) Provide guidelines and safety measures to cautiously handle themselves online and with their cell phones.

(4) As your children grow older, advise them on how to handle peer pressure to do things they aren't comfortable with doing.

(5) Clearly communicate the information in this chapter that outlines the suspicious behaviors of predatory teens and adults that may mean your child is being groomed for assault.

(6) If your child is at home alone after school, make sure they understand they are not to open the door for ANYONE. Any deliveries can be left with a neighbor or on the porch, and anyone trying to "stop by" when you aren't there, even if it's a family member, a friend your

child knows or your pastor, should not be allowed into your home.

Abuse Awareness for Single Mothers

Single parents must also be on alert for adults that will try to get to their child through them. Many single moms are extremely lonely. Desperation for male companionship may motivate them to disregard precautionary vetting of a new man coming into their life and home. Don't be so anxious to have a man or a daddy for your children that you let good common sense fly out the window. You must also not allow your desperation to interfere with legal prosecution of a felon.

The black woman's belief that she is somehow wrong for involving law enforcement in a sexual molestation or assault charge against a black male is common. This erroneous belief stems from the fact that there are great numbers of black men in our criminal justice system and locked up our nation's prisons. I've heard dozens of sad tales about black women throwing their molested daughters out of the house to maintain a relationship with the very man that molested her! As mentioned previously, black women have been brainwashed into believing it is their role to protect grown men from the law because "we already have too many black men in prison!" This is foolish thinking and it must cease.

Never put a man's freedom and peace of mind ahead of a child's. Never feel guilty for taking action to protect the rights of an innocent. It is neither the child's fault nor yours if that man gets locked up for the rest of his life – it's HIS fault! HE is the adult, and the sole party responsible for the actions that will land him in prison. As a man in the community, he is charged with protecting and safekeeping the women and children in said community. Once he abdicates his responsibility, there must be no further allegiance to him.

Whether the man you are dating is a church-going man of God or not is irrelevant; *all* men should be considered suspect until proven otherwise. Your job is to protect your child first and foremost. Mature men, especially those with children of their own, will totally understand and respect your caution and never have a problem with going as slowly as you want before they meet your children.

> (1) If you are dating, watch for men that have a history of dating only single mothers, especially if they the children are all a certain gender and age range;
> (2) Give the side eye to any individual that pressures you to bring your children on outings, that asks more questions about your children than he does you, or requests to meet your children before you mention it. You and getting to know you should be his key focus, not your babies;
> (3) Be suspicious of any adult male that wants to hang around with lots of children instead of adults. There is something wrong with him; and
> (4) Once he does meet your children, never let him babysit, wander around your home and disappear into an area where your child is sleeping or playing alone. Neither should he bathe or change your child, or take pictures of your child unless you are in the photo, too.

Whenever you notice an adult male or older teen that wants to be around your child frequently, who focuses on young children, or pays an unusual amount of attention to youngsters of a specific gender or age group, you should become especially watchful. Black women should not be lulled into a state of unconsciousness nor blinded to the pedophiles and child molesters in their midst, assuming that because a man quotes Scripture or "seems so nice" he couldn't possibly be a freak. The damage done to children emotionally and psychologically from sexual assault can be irreparable.

And as you remind your child about the guidelines set out above, always end by assuring your offspring that your ears, arms and love are always there for them, and that you will do all you can to protect them from harm.

9

THE WOLF IN SHEEP'S CLOTHING FLEECING THE FLOCK

Blacks support their churches with more than $420 billion in tithes and donations. Where does the money go and who controls it?

No one can serve two masters, for either he will hate the one and love the other, or he will be devoted to the one and despise the other. You cannot serve God and money. (Matthew 6:24)

Christianity is Not a Religion, It's an Industry

One of biggest conflicts amongst church-goers of all faiths is whether Scripture mandates that Christians tithe, and if so, how much? Pastors have their favorite quotes designed to induce guilt and open up the pocketbooks of millions of black women. Admittedly, I am no student of divinity, but I am a great researcher. With the possibility that the whole tithing thing was another game being run for the benefit of greedy Christian pastors, I decided to take a closer look at the controversy behind tithing in Scripture and in practice.

Dr. Frank Chase Jr., a Doctor of Theology, has spent more than two years studying the concept and history of tithing. Dr. Chase is adamant about correcting four misconceptions.

(1) Tithing is not money. God never instructed that the tithes had to be 10 percent of your income – tithing references the 10th part of "something."

(2) The New Testament says nothing about you being cursed if you do not tithe.

(3) God never asked for money in any form, not a shekel, silver, gold, coin or anything else.

(4) A tithe references a part of everything from the land grown by the Israelites such as grain, honey, wine, oils, fruit, plots of land, first-born animals, etc.

According to the Bible, tithing does not become a command until Moses' time, and it was, as Dr. Chase describes, related to crop offerings to God for the blessings of rain, and as a tax paid to support the temple and priests. Nowhere in the New

Testament is it mandated that Christians are under any sort of mandatory tithing system for religious purposes. The Old Testament required "a 10th part" of the Levites, but the new covenant does not specify a percentage at all of anyone.

Teachers of tithing suggest that tithing was required by God long before he gave the law to Moses. Quoting Genesis 14:18-20 they preach: *"Then Melchizadek king of Salem brought out bread and wine. He was priest of God Most High, and he blessed Abram saying, 'Blessed be Abram by God Most High, Creator of heaven and earth. And blessed be God Most High, who delivered your enemies into your hand.' Then Abram gave him a tenth of everything"*.

However, when you read the full Scripture, it is apparent that what Abram gave King Melchizadek was not his own property or money at all – he gave over 10 percent of what he recovered in war, returning the other 90 percent to its rightful owners:

[22] And Abram said to the king of Sodom, I have lifted up my hand unto Jehovah, God Most High, possessor of heaven and earth,

[23] that I will not take a thread nor a shoe-latchet nor aught that is thine, lest thou shouldest say, I have made Abram rich:

There is no mention of Abram ever "tithing" again – his own property or anyone else's.

Genesis 28:20-22 is also frequently used to justify Christian tithing of 10 percent. "Then Jacob made a vow, saying, *"If God will be with me and will watch over me on this journey I am taking and will give me food to eat and clothes to wear so that I return safely to my father's house, then the Lord will be my God and this stone that I have set up as a pillar will be God's house, and of all that you give me I will give you a tenth".*

But if you read *exactly* what Jacob said in Genesis 28:20-22, it is very clear that he was making a five-point conditional promise to God that would be fulfilled only:

1. IF God will be with me;
2. IF God will watch over me;
3. IF God will give me food to eat;
4. IF God will give me clothes to wear; and
5. IF I return safely to my father's house

Then, and only then, can God have a tenth of whatever was given to Jacob. Well, Jacob did not return to his father's house for a full 20 years, and there is no written record that he ever fulfilled the conditional promise originally made anyway.

Dr. Chase's research is in accord with that of L. Ray Smith of Bible-Truths.Org, who has also spent years researching the validity of tithing. Mr. Smith's language is a bit more colorful, but very clearly reflective of the thinking of millions of Christians as they wake up to the pimp game of mandated tithing:

> "On any given Sunday morning there will be numerous men-of-the-cloth who will be bellowing out over the air waves that people are being "cursed with a curse" because they have failed to pay God 10 percent of their paychecks. And should such a gullible listener decide to repent and give God 10 percent of his salary, just how would he do that? Just keep reading. These men of the cloth who often have

unquenchable worldly desires of the flesh, will be sure to give you an address where you can send them (or, ah, rather God) your tithe. And do they have a right to quote these Scriptures in this manner? No they do not, and furthermore they themselves know better."

Intrigued by their information (which so greatly varied from the messages received in church that we MUST tithe10 percent or we have cheated and sinned against God), I put together a list of about a dozen misconceptions Christian black women have about tithing, culled from a variety of resources which include a Jewish rabbi.

- Only farmers and those in the animal husbandry business were required to tithe. Carpenters, bakers, shop keepers, hunters, fishermen, writers, poets, tent-makers, educators, wine makers, candle makers, metal workers, fabric and clothing producers, etc. did not and were not required to tithe the wages they earned.
- Money was never mentioned in the Bible as a tithable commodity. If a farmer or herder lived far away, he might sell his sheep then convert the money to food or animals closer to the temple/meeting place rather than herd them long distances.
- If a herder owned less than 10 animals, he was not required to tithe. Neither was what was called "the righteous poor" who had no animals or crops of their own.
- Jesus did not teach the disciples or anyone else about tithing. Christ makes two statements about tithing to the Pharisees, but neither says that *the Disciples of Christ*

should tithe anything nor are they to receive tithes. All other mentions of tithing are found in the Law of Moses.

- Abraham voluntarily tithed exactly one time, and he did not tithe his own personal property, crops or livestock. There is no record of Abraham or Jacob tithing weekly or ever again in the Bible.

- Only Levite priests (descendants of the sons of Aaron) could collect tithes at temple, and there are no Levite priests or temples today. Jews (the Israelites that are the subject of discussion in the Scriptures on tithing), do not even pay tithes to their temples! **"There is no longer an obligation to support the Levites and Priests as they are no longer working in the Temple.** *Rabbis are normally supported by the contributions of their congregants through their Synagogue membership."* ~ Rabbi Reuven Lauffer, Jerusalem

- Tithes were not something that you turned over to anyone else – they were used for the good of a group of people and consumed. Deu.14:22-23 (God's commandment to the Israelites) *"You shall truly tithe all the increase... year by year. And YOU SHALL EAT before the Lord your God... the TITHE of your grain and your new wine... that you may learn to fear the Lord your God always."* The Israelites were mandated to take their tithes to an appointed location. Tithes were consumed in a religious feast celebrating God, communing with family, servants, Levites and travelers.

- Every third year the tribes of Israel were commanded to bring their tithes to storehouses on tribal lands for the Levites (descendants of Levi who served as teachers and rabbis), as well as travelers, fatherless children and widows so that they could come and get food. Live animals would be kept by the Levites and killed for meat as needed, milked for cheese, etc. (Deuteronomy 14:27–29) *"You shall not forsake the Levite... at the end of EVERY THIRD YEAR you shall BRING THE TITHE of your produce of THAT YEAR and store it up WITHIN YOUR GATES. And the LEVITE, and the FATHERLESS and the WIDOW... may come and eat and be satisfied, that the Lord your God may BLESS YOU in all the work of your hand which you do."*

- Another Scripture often quoted to induce Christian congregations to tithe is Mal 3:8-10 KJV *"Will a man rob God? Yet ye have robbed me. But ye say, Wherein have we robbed thee? In tithes and offerings. Ye are cursed with a curse: for ye have robbed me, even this whole nation. Bring ye all the tithes into the storehouse, that there may be meat in mine house, and prove me now herewith, saith the LORD of hosts, if I will not open you the windows of heaven, and pour you out a blessing, that there shall not be room enough to receive it."* Jesus was admonishing the Levite priests who were under the mandate to share their tithes with the ministering priests and the poor, instead of keeping most for themselves. Again, black women are not Levite priests, not descendants of Levi and not under any mandate to tithe.
- Neither Jesus Christ, or his Disciples Peter and Paul collected or gave tithes, because they were not Levites either (being descended from the tribe of Judah). If the most holy of men were able to preach the Gospel without biblical tithes, certainly black preachers can do the same! Preachers have created their own version of tithing laws that are not supported by the Bible at all.

- Though Mal 3:8-10 KJV is used to stir fear and guilt in church-going black women, it is impossible for Christians to rob God, as God has not transferred or given a tithe law to Christians. Without Levites and priests doing service in the temple, paying a tithe is a "sin" both to the giver and the receiver. Jewish rabbis are adamant that obeying God's law means we are not to pay a tithe unless we pay it to the ones ordained by God to accept that tithe.
- Christians receive blessings from God for having Christ as their Savior and not by any application of the Old Covenant laws which means no payment of tithes are required for you to be blessed by God or gain entrance to Heaven.
- In the New Testament tithe and tithing are referenced about seven times (Matthew 23:23; Luke 11:42; 18:12; Hebrews 7:5-6,8-9). Apostle Paul states that believers should set aside a portion of their income in order to support the church, but it's very clear that the amount should be "in keeping with income" (1 Corinthians 16:2)

Somehow Scriptures from both the Old and New Covenants got translated by greed or illiterate preachers (not sure which), and communicated to parishioners as a "10 percent mandatory minimum" amount to tithe monthly to churches. This is flatly a lie designed to pimp you out of your money.

"Now then, is there a scholar alive anywhere on earth that can explain to us how this one, single, unparalleled and never-again-to-be-duplicated event is Scriptural proof that Christians should give 10 percent of their annual salaries (not the spoils of war, but their money, their salaries), not once, but year after year after year, not to Melchizedek, but to Clergymen who claim to be ministers of Jesus Christ? If anyone can see a similarity here, I will show him the similarity between an elephant and a fruit fly." (L. Ray Smith)

In light of the information set out above, it is my opinion that no church should ever be given a tithe, just voluntary donations of time in service, and money **as a member is able.** In accordance with 2 Corinthians 9:7 *Each man should give what he has decided in his heart to give, not reluctantly or under compulsion, for God loves a cheerful giver.* Giving does not have to be in monetary form.

Tithing can be the time you spend at a senior center twice per week playing the piano and singing songs. It may be volunteering as a Girl Scout or Boy Scout leader for children in your community. Maybe you are a hairdresser that saves donates three spots a week for women from a battered woman's shelter that need a makeover so they can find a job. Perhaps you shop for two families when you buy groceries at Costco, and split your giant packages of food and cases of canned goods with a single parent in your building that works hard, but is still struggling to feed her children.

What matters most is that all offerings be given freely, not with an attitude of expected return on your investment ("seed faith"). Giving should not be of service to the pastor, but to the poor. Nothing should be given to impress members of your church with your pew position, based on the amount of tithes paid.

> *"My people have become lost sheep; their shepherds have led them astray. They have made them turn aside on the mountains; they have gone along from mountain to hill and have forgotten their resting place."*
> *(Jeremiah 50:6)*

Prosperity ministers popular in black churches grow fat and rich by preaching unbiblical promises of prosperity to desperately poor black women and their fatherless children. It is a shameful misuse of Scripture for black preachers to twist the words of the Bible to manipulate women and children to give to them, when the church is mandated by Scripture to care for those that God seeks to protect. The poor, the homeless, fatherless children, and the widows of deceased men have always been the focus of God (Deuteronomy 14:28-29, 24:17-22; Exodus 23:11; and Psalm 12:5, 72:4, 11-12).

In closing, in 4000 years of recorded biblical history there is not a single example of what churches practice today, mandating that their Christian church members tithe money from their income. The New Testament has nothing about tithing money to a church, or tithing regularly period. And in the Old Testament, all tithing was in consumable goods required for the personal needs, survival and nourishment of God's people – that's it!

Church members must also correct their thinking about tithing and finances. Some black churches preach that if a member encounters financial difficulties, it must be because that person was not tithing, or that they haven't been tithing the full 10 percent required. This is faulty thinking. Christians are admonished to share and give, be faithful and fair in their dealings. One cannot erase the requirements of the latter by writing a check. Paying a tithe does nothing to eliminate responsibility to one's fellow man, which includes one's nuclear and extended family, fellow church members, immediate neighborhood, and greater community.

> *"But if any provide not for his own, and especially for those of his own house, he hath denied the faith, and is worse than AN INFIDEL"* (1st Timothy 5:8).

There is no excuse for a church to have millions of dollars in its coffers, with hungry or cold children or seniors right down the street. With a mega-church in its midst, there should never be people sick due to their inability to afford prescribed medication. With hundreds of black churches in a city, there should be no black parents that are desperate to get job training, or they can't move up because they cannot afford to pay employment-related educational expenses on their minimum-wage salary. There is just no excuse for the greed of black pastors that drive through ramshackle neighborhoods of desperate people to arrive at their churches in $75,000 cars, or going on a Caribbean vacation in their private Lear jet.

> *"He who gives to the poor will lack nothing, but he who closes his eyes to them receives many curses".* (Proverbs 28:27)

Sociologists and scholars of the prosperity ministry have expressed concerns about why it is that low-income, disadvantaged, and disenfranchised people seem so drawn to non-scriptural prosperity gospel that leaves them broke but makes their preachers millionaires. No one prospers from prosperity gospel but the preachers collecting your money!

Black women seem to find hope, even a source of pride, in a pastor who preaches prosperity and lives a flamboyant lifestyle, while they volunteer their meager funds to his church and live in abject poverty with their children. This is the exact same mindset of the ho that suffers indignities and abuse to buy her pimp a Rolls Royce, fur coats, diamonds and gold. The pimp dresses in custom-tailored suits while the ho wears polyester clothing from Walmart. The similarities in thinking cannot be ignored.

"He that oppresseth the poor to increase his riches, and he that giveth to the rich, shall surely come to want." (Proverbs 22:16)

Pastor Arranged Marriages for Profit

While researching and interviewing for this book, I heard dozens of stories of Pastors setting women up with their friends to be pimped in arranged marriages. In this scenario, pastor's friend is always some broke down scallywag N.A.M. (Nothing Ass Man), that just happens to attend his church. The woman is an educated, financially solvent woman that owns her own home and gives generously to the church. Even if he hasn't seen her W-2 form, the pastor has an idea of her annual income and knows his buddy is gonna come up big time by marrying this lonely woman.

The game begins by gaining control of the female congregation's minds to make them desperate for marriage. What pastor has not attempted to shore up the morale of his congregation of females by reminding them that "a man that finds a wife finds a good thing?" (Proverbs 18:22). So wouldn't it make sense that a single woman would be desirous of being that blessed thing to a man? She would most likely seek to date a

Christian man so that she would have the opportunity to marry and create the family the Scriptures find favor with, right? Enter the pastor to save the day.

Lauding his friend as Saved and a good Christian man suitable for marriage, the pastor arranges a meeting. A single woman is set up to become a victim by being told that this is the man she has prayed for and that God has finally sent him to her life. He is a good man, pastor says, and because he is of the body of Christ, they are equally yoked under the eyes of God. She is courted for a few months, an engagement is announced, and soon she is married. The man moves into her nice, well-appointed home since he doesn't have a pot to piss in or a window to throw it out of. Shortly after the honeymoon, the drama begins.

First, her new husband demands that she add his name to the deed of her home and to all of her bank accounts. Most women with good sense will say "no!" This is when the pastor steps in and instructs the woman that she must submit. She is warned that her resistance to sharing assets is preventing her husband from being the head of his household as the Lord has ordained.

Though a little voice inside is telling her that she shouldn't listen to pastor, her desire to be a good wife to the husband she has prayed for wins out, so she reluctantly complies. Two years later she has no money in her accounts and her home is in danger of foreclosure. She's in debt up to her eyeballs after she co-signed on the loans he needed to start his new business. When the business failed due to mismanagement and laziness, he blamed her for not believing in him and supporting his dreams.

The man that was so loving and attentive before marriage is now cruel, cold and abusive. She can't believe that she waited and prayed years and years for this as she cries herself to sleep every night. All the pastor has to say now about the situation is "I'll pray for you."

Mega-Church = Mo Money, Mo Money, Mo Money!

Churches used to be the source of community in black neighborhoods – everyone knew the other members of the church, and fellowshipping was an integral part of the worship. With the advent of mega-churches, such bonding and sense of community were replaced with social status; to be a member of a popular mega-church is viewed in some circles as an important status symbol.

Though many churches boast a large membership, they do not qualify as a mega-church. The Hartford Institute for Religion Research (http://hirr.hartsem.edu) describes a megachurch in the following manner:

> "The term megachurch is the name given to a cluster of very large, Protestant congregations, which share several distinctive characteristics. These churches generally have:
>
> 2000 or more persons in attendance at weekly worship
> A charismatic, authoritative senior minister
> A very active 7-day-a-week congregational community
> A multitude of social and outreach ministries
> A complex differentiated organizational structure"

Mega-churches pull in some serious coin which is demonstrated using some very rough financial estimates. Let's say a church has regular traffic of 10,000 visitors weekly. If those 10,000 people were credited with just a $5.00 donation (which we know is extremely low), that's a total take of $50,000 per week. Multiplied by 52 weeks in a year, we are looking at a minimum take of $2.6 million annually. With 10 percent tithing, building fund donations, Pastor Love Offerings, and double or triple collection plate offerings, it's easy to see how a mega church can easily pull in $6-10 million per year. The Lakewood Church in Houston, Texas where Joel Osteen preaches has a reported yearly budget of more than $80 million (as much or more than many small American cities). But where is the money mega-churches take in? And in largely black congregations, what good is being done for black women and children in the communities in which these churches stand?

"Though I understand that some people tend to be drawn to things they feel are popular with others, and especially that are on television, I don't understand the need for mega churches with upwards of 5,000 members or more. What are folks thinking? Who's getting the collection plate from that and who handles the tithes? Why do the pastor and his wife live like a king and queen while folks sign a contract with the church to pay a 10th of their earnings (tithes)? How is that helping the individual to get rich? Granted some of these churches do offer financial counseling and banking services from what I've heard, but with churches having the reputation of crooks running off with people's money, I don't trust them. Bottom line, black folks need to stop using the church as a crutch to fix what they need to work on themselves inside." ~D. Bell

Even more unbelievable is a recent story about Apostle Fred Price, one of the biggest names in the Prosperity Ministry. According to comments made by posters (verified by taking a peek at the related website which you can see at www.jcmedia.cc/ficwfm//credit), Pimp Price is asking for donations to start a privately owned credit union. His inspiring message to get you to write a check: *"Now the multitude of those who believed were of one heart and one soul; neither did anyone say that any of the things he possessed was his own, but they had all things in common."* (Acts 4:32)

What?

Pushing the FICWFM credit union as a wealth-building tool for the body of Christ, poor people are giving Price money to make him even wealthier with no expectation of getting anything for it. Videos on the website announced that the original opening date was May 2011. However, across the top of the home page of the website is a one line notice of delay that reads *"The FICWFM Credit Union was scheduled to open previously; however, the credit union opening date has been delayed. We will notify you of a new date.* An Inspirational Initiative of Dr. Frederick K. C. Price." I corrected the two typographical errors present in just one sentence.

Another video clip shows Pimp Price's sidekicks talking about "None Suffer Lack" by pooling our resources together everyone will have plenty. With all of these guys qualifying as multi-

213

millionaires, why can't they pool THEIR resources and start the credit union?

There is also a legal disclaimer which serves as notice that you better NOT even think about getting a dime for the money you send Pimp Price. Essentially you are making a voluntary donation to a rich man so he can use your money to help him get richer. Even if the unchartered credit union dream never becomes a reality, you have no legal recourse, no way to get your "donation" back, and nothing to show for the money you've given him.

> **"Legal Disclaimer**
> I understand that this donation is to support the establishment of the FICWFM Credit Union, which is not chartered at this time. It will not be used to establish membership or to establish any account or other benefit for me. The opportunity for my financial participation in the credit union, as a member with all benefits thereto, will be presented at a future time."

For those that do not know, chartered financial institutions such as banks, savings and loans, and credit unions are normally started with seed money put up by investors that expect to get a tidy return on their investment.

Banks can petition the government to have their depositors accounts insured for up to $500,000 by the Federal Deposit Insurance Corporation (FDIC). This insurance policy protects account holders money should the bank go belly up or the bank's cash reserves dip below set levels. Credit unions are federally insured up to $250,000 per account by another governmental agency, the National Credit Union Administration (NCUA) for the same purposes.

In this instance Price has made no such promises, there is no return offered, and "donations" do not entitle a congregant to any legal claim or rights to profits generated by the credit union. Neither does the money sent to Price go into an account of any kind for future use by the sender. And since the credit union is unchartered, it does not qualify for NCUA account insurance, so if there were a financial problem, there is no guarantee that a depositor would get their money back anyway. Finally, FICWFM's unchartered status means that neither Price nor his "board" can be charged with bank fraud for keeping the money sent to them.

Several people have written to tell me that their churches have begun demanding that members submit copies of their W-2 forms. Shocked at this blatant invasion of privacy, but still seeking blessings from Jesus, they complied with the request. I imagine the churches are calling for these documents to verify that parishioners are tithing a full 10 percent of their actual gross income.

The greed of the pulpit pimp knows no bounds.

CONCLUSION

Putting it All Together

*The most common way women give up
their power is by thinking they don't have any.
~ Alice Walker*

Christianity, Islam, Judaism and many of the other so-called religions of this earth have kept women in bondage for thousands of years, using the alleged "word of God" to do so. It seems ironic and some sort of twisted logic that women would seek salvation through the same patriarchal belief systems that put them in bondage in the first place. Women fill the pews of most churches, with black women (statistically the most religious demographic in the nation), leading the pack. Have you ever noticed that the most oppressed peoples around the globe are all very religious? Haven't you ever asked yourself why?

Being a person who has, since early childhood, felt very uneasy with religious dogma, I've often wondered why it seemed that I stood alone in questioning something most black folks accepted without concern. A precocious child, the hypocrisy, guilt tactics and obvious fear and hatred of women evident in the black church was obvious even at the tender age of eight. I'd enjoyed Sunday school, but then I started asking questions. I asked questions that my Sunday school teacher didn't know the answer to, or he provided derisive answers I felt were dismissive of my intellect based upon the fact that I was a female. Resistant even in childhood of allowing men in church to define who I was or what I was to think, feel or say, I decided that church was not for me. So I never went back.

The fact that I made the correct decision was reinforced when I reached high school. Boys were quick to tell the girls what we were "supposed" to do or not do, and that they were "supposed" to be the head of everything (including us), because the Bible said so. As I grew into my 20s and 30s, I heard black men reiterate the same guilt-blaming rhetoric that made black women responsible for all that was wrong with men, with families, and with black society in general. When I again asked "Why is that?" there never seemed to be any answer other than "that's just the way it is, God said so, and you need to get with the program."

Black women in churches are socialized to believe that men are more important than women and children, and that we are mandated by God to define ourselves as mere helpers to black men. When are black women going to recognize that the structure of the traditional black church provides a false sense of comfort while they are subjected to nothing but suffering and domination by black men?

For some reason, black women hang on their Bibles and the churches they've attended (often for decades) for dear life. There is a great deal of fear associated with being fully self reliant, fully accountable human beings that strike out and find their own way in the world. In churches across the country, the black woman's predilection for a spiritual connection with the world and others is being used as a weapon to keep you in check, as it is black people as a whole.

Black women must stop allowing yourselves to be lulled into believing that you have no rights to demand to be treated with respect. You have the right to expect that you will not be used for sex, for your money, for free housing, for your cooking skills, for rides in your car while you "help" or "save" sorry men. You have not been placed on this earth to be the sole source of comfort for the black man's fragile ego. You are here to be a self-actualizing, wondrous spirit of life that walks in the warmth of the light cast by the sun, moon and stars!

As long as black women allow themselves to be dazzled by fast-talking black men and their weapon of religion, we will always be at the bottom, fruitlessly working to save the black man and the black community by ourselves. Just like King Sisyphus of Greek mythology who was cursed for eternity to push a boulder up a hill, only to have it roll back down to the bottom. Every morning Sisyphus was forced to start all over again performing a useless and repetitive task. Imagine the energy expended in such pointless efforts, accomplishing nothing day in and day out? Black women indoctrinated in church-related gender roles believe that they must "save" the black man; thus a lot of female energy, effort and money are expended working toward a goal for which you will receive no reward.

Black women have also been socialized to see African-American men as their singular choice in a mate. Black women need to open their eyes to the wide range of men on this planet interested in loving, honoring and raising a family with them. Men all over the world appreciate the unique beauty and strong heart that is you. It is not wrong for you to think of the life you want to create for yourself and your children, and to execute that plan independent of black men.

Prepare yourself, however, for the pushback: Black men frightened of losing their power base and hold over you will accuse you of being a lesbian man-hater, of turning your back on black men, of dismantling the black family and abandoning the black community. This is nothing but circular, double-talking pimp game and gender blaming. In reality the black community *is* you and your children, and the sole parties responsible for abandoning and destroying the black family and community are immoral black men – the men you've submitted to and followed right into the depths of despair.

The path to true enlightenment has been shown to black women repeatedly; it is obvious that such a path does not lead to mega-churches, tithing or preachers of prosperity gospel. Church leaders have proven themselves to be undeserving of your devotion or of your respect, and most certainly undeserving of your money.

Religious men will use the Bible and its texts to hold women responsible for everything they do and feel that they deem to be negative or that frightens them, thus making women responsible for male thoughts and behavior. Rather than accept that men alone are responsible for their choices -- their adultery, their fornication and their sex addictions -- they blame women. The time has come for us to break free of the confining chains of black men and their pimp game of religion. Such churches and church leaders do nothing but stand in the way of African-American women achieving a true spiritual connection with their Creator.

Though your neighborhood black church may hold sentimental value, there comes a time when one must reexamine habits and beliefs, choosing a new path when it becomes obvious that the old one is not bringing you the results you seek. If you've been participating in your church for 10, 12, 18 years looking for love and a husband to make your life complete, and you haven't found him yet, it's time to try something new. If you've been attending a church rocked by scandalous behaviors that have harmed the members in any way, or if you or your children have been victimized or feel unsafe, it's time to try something new.

I prayed for twenty years but received no answer until I prayed with my legs. ~Frederick Douglass

Stand up sistah! There is a huge world out here full of men of many different religious and spiritual beliefs, races, cultures and ages. Traditional thinking about women, men and gender roles that place black women in a small box is passé – this is 2012! Break free of the chains of mental control promoted by the black church and look around! Broaden your horizons and explore other options for romance and spiritual enlightenment. Follow your heart and do what works for you.

In the 1933 masterpiece *Miseducation of the Negro* scholar Carter G. Woodson discussed the black church and its place in the changing African-American community. Though his comments were general in nature, modifying them to focus on females will illustrate my point:

> *"The Negro [females], however, will not advance far if they continue to waste their energy on those who misdirect and exploit*

them. The exploiters of the race are not so much at fault as the race itself. If Negro [females] persist in permitting themselves to be handled in this fashion they will always find some one at hand to impose upon them. The matter is one which rests largely with the Negro [females] themselves. The race will free itself from exploiters as soon as it decides to do so. No one else can accomplish this task for the race. It must plan and do for itself."

Black churches and the men running them certainly have a vested interest in maintaining high numbers of single black women and their children as members of their congregations. However, you don't have to become one of their victims nor a part of those sad statistics.

It's time for black women to roll up our sleeves and begin doing the work that is going to save us and our children, as it has become apparent that neither Jesus nor the black man is going to do it for us.

About The Author

Deborrah Cooper gained underground acclaim through her 18-year career of web-based relationship advice counseling, conducting seminars and workshops in the San Francisco Bay Area and as a producer and host of "HeartBeat," a cable television talk show aired in Oakland, California. She was a frequent on-air guest at KMEL 106.1 radio and guest columnist on AOL's NetNoir channel. Since 2007 she's hosted and produced *The Date Smarter Not Harder Relationships Talk Show* on the BlogTalkRadio Network.

Ms. Cooper has been featured in Black Enterprise magazine, and interviewed for CNN.Com, Ebony, Essence, Honey, Jet, and Downtown Oakland magazines, The Dallas Morning News, The Oakland Tribune, and many other regional and international publications and websites. She has also appeared as a guest expert on the nationally broadcast Tom Joyner Morning Show, The Michael Baisden Show, The Al Sharpton Show, The Michael Eric Dyson show, and featured on BET Television's 'Oh Drama!'

Deborrah writes a dating advice column for the S.F. Examiner, serving as the San Francisco Dating Advice Examiner. Writing under the moniker 'Ms. HeartBeat,' she has penned hundreds of articles and provided advice to thousands on her popular blog Surviving Dating.Com, and the groundbreaking AskHeartBeat.Com website. Launched in 1997, AskHeartBeat is one of the longest running 100% Black owned websites on the Internet, and the first to focus exclusively on Black male/female and interracial relationships. Follow Deborrah on Twitter @msheartbeat.

In religion and politics, people's beliefs and convictions are in almost every case gotten second-hand, and without examination.

~Mark Twain

Bibliography

Article: Abel, G., Becker, J., Cunningham-Rathner, J. *Complications, consent, and cognitions in sex between children and adults.* International Journal of Law and Psychiatry, 7, 89-103 (1984)

Article: Periela, Ariela, *The Biblical Character Jezebel.* About.Com Judaism (www.judaism.about.com/od/jewishpersonalities/a/Who-Was-Jezebel-Bible.htm)

Article: LiveSteenz Research Report *Were is the $420 Billion in Tithes and Offerings The Black Church Has Received Since 1980?* (www.livesteez.com/news/read/Where-is-the-420-Billion-in-Tithes-and-Offerings-the-Black-Church-has-Received-Since-1980/2051.html)

Article: *African American Church History Timeline.* A project of Christian Timelines.Com (www.christiantimelines.com/aa_church.htm)

Article: *'These Boots are Made for Walking': Why Most Divorce Filers Are Women.* Brinig, M.F. and Allen, D.W. *Am Law Econ Rev (2000) 2(1): 126-169 doi:10.1093/aler/2.1.126*

Andersen, Donna and Walfish, Dr. Fran. *Interview on The Date Smarter Not Harder Relationships Talk Show entitled "Dating a Sociopath: How to Recognize a Sociopath in Your Life Before You Get Hurt"* (November 20, 2011) (www.survivingdating.com/young-men-being-raised-to-be-sociopaths)

Barna Research Group, *"20 Years of Surveys Show Key Differences in the Faith of America's Men and Women"*. State of the Church Series (2011) www.barna.org

Bradley, Anthony (2012). *Keep Your Head Up: America's New Black Christian Leaders, Social Consciousness, and the Cosby Conversation.* Crossway Books.

Brent, Linda (Harriet Ann Jacobs) (1861) *Incidents in the Life of a Slave Girl Written by Herself.* Second edition, 2003 ca. 550K Academic Affairs Library, UNC-CH (http://docsouth.unc.edu/fpn/jacobs/jacobs.html

Camara, Jeremiah (2004). *Holy Lockdown: Does the Church Limit Black Progress?* Twelfth House Publishing

Carle, Graeme (3rd Ed. 2000) *Eating Sacred Cows, A Closer Look at Tithing,* (New Zealand) Emmanus Road Publishing

Guttmacher Institute, *US Teen Pregnancies, Births and Abortions: National and State Trends and Trends by Race and Ethnicity,* January 2010

Crawford, Evans E. (1995). *The Hum: Call and Response in African American Preaching.* Abington Press.

Evans, Patricia (2010). *The Verbally Abusive Relationship: How to Recognize It and How to Respond.* Adams Media

Franklin, Robert M. (2007). *Crisis in the Village: Restoring Hope in African American Communities.* Fortress Press

Entrapping the Innocent: Toward a Theory of Child Sexual Predators' Luring Communication (2007). Loreen N. Olson, Joy L. Daggs, Barbara L.

Ellevold, Teddy K. K. Rogers. Communication Theory Vol 17, Issue 3, pages 231–251

Freire, Paulo. *Pedagogy of the Oppressed*. New York: Continuum International Publishing Group, Inc., 2000.

Hardy III, Clarence E. *James Baldwin's God: Sex, Hope, and Crisis in Black Holiness Culture*. Knoxville: The University of Tennessee Press, 2003.

hooks, bell. *Feminist Theory: From Margin to Center*. Second Edition. Cambridge, MA: South End Press, 1984, 2000.

hooks, bell. *Ain't I a Woman: Black Women and Feminism*. Boston, MA: South End Press, 1981.

Kelley, Russell Earl. (2007) *Should the Church Teach Tithing? A Theologians Conclusions of a Taboo Doctrine* New York. Writers Club Press.

Lincoln, C. Eric and Mamiya, Lawrence H. (1990) *The Black Church in the African American Experience* (Durham: Duke University Press)

Milner, Christina and Richard (1972). *Black Players: The Secret World of Black Pimps*. Little, Brow and Company, Boston.

Mitchell, Henry H. (2004). *Black Church Beginnings: The Long-Hidden Realities of The First Years*. Grand Rapids, Michigan: Wm. B. Eerdsmans Publishing Company

Morrow, David (2005) *Why Men Hate Going to Church* Nashville, TN., Thomas Nelson, Inc.

National Campaign to Prevent Teen Pregnancy, *Not Just Another Single Issue: Teen Pregnancy, Out of Wedlock Births, and Marriage*, 2002

The National Intimate Partner and Sexual Violence Study (2010) published by the National Center for Injury Prevention and Control (http://www.cdc.gov/violenceprevention/NISVS/index.html)

National Victim Center (1992) and Crime Victims Treatment and Research Center - Rape in America: A Report to the Nation. Arlington, Va. (www.musc.edu/ncvc/resources_prof/rape_in_america.pdf)

Pagelow, M.D. (1981b). *Sex roles, power, and woman battering*. In Women and crime in America. Bowker, L.H. (ed.) New York: MacMillan

Pagelow, M.D., & Johnson, (1988). *Abuse in the American Family*. In Abuse and religion: When praying isn't enough. Horton, A.L., and Williamson, J.A. (eds.) Lexington, Mass: Lexington Books.

PEW Research Center (January 2009) "A Religious Portrait of African Americans". The PEW Research Center Forum on Religion and Public Life. Washington, D.C.

Religiosity and teen birth rate in the United States. Strayhorn, Richard M. and Strayhorn, Jillian C. Reprod Health. 2009; 6: 14. (www.ncbi.nlm.nih.gov/pmc/articles/PMC2758825/?tool=pubmed)

Ross, Rick, Intervention Specialist. Warning Signs of a Potentially Unsafe Group/Leader at www.rickross.com/warningsigns.html.

Sexual Abuse of Boys: Definition, Prevalence, Correlates, Sequelae, and Management. William C. Holmes, MD, MSCE; Gail B. Slap, MD, MS.

Journal of The American Medical Association, JAMA. 1998;280(21):1855-1862.

Smith, L. Ray, Bible-Truths.Org at www.bible-truths.org.

Wardell J. Payne (1995), *Directory of African American Religious Bodies: A Compendium by the Howard University School of Divinity* (Washington, DC: Howard University Press).

Other Sources

The Pied Piper of Hamelin, as told by Daryll Bellingham, storyteller at http://www.storytell.com.au/stories/PiedPiper.html

Printed in Great Britain
by Amazon